Nutrition and Immune Health

Gabriella Goldberger

Published by Azure Time Press, 2023.

NUTRITION AND IMMUNE HEALTH

First edition. September 7, 2023.

ISBN: 979-8215291252

Written by Gabriella Goldberger.

Also by Gabriella Goldberger

Mindful Eating: Nourish Your Well-Being
Holistic Approaches to Stress Management
Nutrition and Immune Health
The Connection Between Sleep and Health

Table of Contents

Chapter 1: Introduction to Nutrition and Immune Health...................................1

Chapter 3: Gut Health and Immunity... 26

Chapter 4: Inflammation and Immune Responses 38

Chapter 5: Building a Strong Immune Foundation in Childhood 51

Chapter 6: Immune-Boosting Diets and Eating Patterns........................... 62

Chapter 7: Nutritional Strategies for Aging Gracefully 73

Chapter 8: Food Safety and Immunity 84

Chapter 9: Immune-Boosting Supplements and Their Controversies 96

Chapter 10: Putting Knowledge into Practice: Meal Plans and Recipes 108

To all those who strive to nourish their bodies and nurture their immune health,

May this book serve as your trusted companion on your journey to better well-being. Your dedication to making positive choices for your immune health inspires us all.

With gratitude,

Gabriella Goldberger

Chapter 1: Introduction to Nutrition and Immune Health

Understanding the Immune System's Role in Protecting the Body

The immune system serves as your body's guardian, constantly vigilant and ready to defend against a myriad of potential threats. It's a highly intricate network, comprising cells, tissues, and proteins that collaborate seamlessly to detect and eliminate harmful pathogens such as viruses, bacteria, and other invaders. This immune defense mechanism is akin to having an army of microscopic superheroes always on duty to safeguard your well-being.

To comprehend the profound connection between nutrition and immune health, we must first grasp the intricacies of the immune system's functions.

The Immune System: A Multi-Layered Shield

The immune system is not a monolithic entity but a dynamic and multi-layered defense system. Picture it as your body's dedicated security team, perpetually operating on high alert to ensure your safety.

At its core, the immune system consists of two primary lines of defense: the innate immune system and the adaptive immune system. These two arms of immunity complement each other to provide comprehensive protection against a wide range of pathogens.

Innate Immune System

The innate immune system acts as a rapid-response team, providing immediate, albeit general, protection against a wide array of threats. This initial line of defense includes physical barriers like your skin and mucous membranes, which act as formidable fortresses, preventing pathogens from entering your body. Beyond these physical defenses, innate immunity also encompasses various types of white blood cells, such as phagocytes and natural killer cells. These immune warriors can swiftly identify and neutralize invaders, serving as the initial barricade against potential threats.

Adaptive Immune System

In contrast, the adaptive immune system operates as your body's precision strike force. It may take more time to activate, but it offers the advantage of long-term protection. This sophisticated system "remembers" previous encounters with pathogens, enabling it to produce highly specific antibodies and immune cells designed to target those particular invaders. This adaptive memory is the reason why, after recovering from certain diseases or receiving vaccinations, you develop immunity and are less likely to become ill from the same pathogen in the future.

The Dynamic Dance of Immunity

The immune system is in a constant state of alertness, ready to respond to potential threats at a moment's notice. It operates through a dynamic and intricate dance of cellular communication and signaling pathways. Think of it as an orchestra, with each immune cell and molecule playing a unique role in maintaining harmony within your body.

White blood cells, such as lymphocytes and macrophages, are the principal actors in this immunological symphony. When a pathogen enters your body, it's akin to a foreign note disrupting the melody. The immune system detects this disturbance and sets off a cascade of events to neutralize the threat. This may involve the production of antibodies, which are proteins that specifically target the invader, or the recruitment of immune cells to engulf and eliminate the pathogen.

The Role of Nutrition in Immune Function

Now that we have a foundational understanding of the immune system's role in protecting the body, it's crucial to recognize that this intricate defense mechanism relies on a variety of nutrients and compounds to function optimally. In essence, your immune system is only as strong as the building blocks you provide it. It's like equipping your security team with the best tools and equipment to ensure they can perform their duties effectively.

Questions for Reflection:

1. Have you ever wondered how your body knows when it's under attack from harmful invaders?
2. What do you think distinguishes the innate immune system from the adaptive immune system in terms of their functions?
3. How might your dietary choices impact the performance of your immune system?
4. Can you think of any specific nutrients or foods that could potentially boost your immune system's capabilities?
5. How does the immune system maintain a delicate balance between protecting the body and not overreacting to harmless substances?

The Impact of Nutrition on Immune System Function

Your immune system's performance is intrinsically linked to the nutrients and compounds you provide through your diet. Think of it as the fuel that powers your body's defenders—the better the fuel, the stronger and more efficient your immune system becomes.

Nutrients as the Building Blocks of Immunity

Imagine your immune system as a well-structured fortress, with each component playing a specific role in defense. The nutrients you consume serve as the building blocks for this fortress. Without the right materials, it becomes challenging to maintain the integrity and strength of your immune defenses.

Let's take a closer look at some essential nutrients and their roles:

1. Vitamins: The Immune System's Allies

Vitamins, such as vitamin C, D, and E, are crucial for immune function. They act as potent antioxidants, neutralizing harmful free radicals that can damage immune cells. Vitamin C, in particular, is known for its ability to support the production and function of immune cells. Vitamin D plays a role in regulating immune responses, while vitamin E helps protect cell membranes.

2. Minerals: The Mighty Supporters

Minerals like zinc are indispensable for immune health. Zinc is involved in various immune processes, including the development and function of immune cells. It helps maintain the integrity of your skin and mucous membranes, which are essential barriers against pathogens.

3. Protein: The Body's Repair Crew

Protein is not only essential for muscle building but also for the production of antibodies and immune cells. These molecules are like the frontline soldiers of your immune system, constantly patrolling and neutralizing threats. Ensuring an adequate intake of high-quality protein is crucial for maintaining a robust immune response.

4. Phytonutrients: The Immune Superheroes

Phytonutrients are compounds found in plant-based foods, such as fruits, vegetables, and herbs. They are known for their immune-boosting properties. For example, flavonoids in fruits and vegetables have antioxidant and anti-inflammatory effects, supporting immune cell function. Curcumin, found in turmeric, has potent anti-inflammatory properties, while garlic contains allicin, known for its antimicrobial effects.

5. Water: The Hydration Hero

Proper hydration is often overlooked but is crucial for maintaining immune function. Water helps transport nutrients to immune cells and aids in the removal of waste products. Dehydration can weaken the immune system and impair its ability to respond effectively to threats.

Balanced Nutrition: The Key to a Resilient Immune System

To optimize immune function, it's not about one single nutrient but rather the synergy of various nutrients working together. A balanced diet that includes a wide variety of foods ensures you receive the necessary nutrients to fortify your immune defenses.

Questions for Reflection:

1. How do you currently ensure you're getting a variety of vitamins and minerals in your diet?
2. Are there any specific foods or supplements you rely on to support your immune system?
3. Have you noticed any changes in your health when you've had periods of nutrient-rich versus nutrient-poor diets?
4. What are some strategies you can implement to enhance your overall nutrient intake?
5. How does the impact of nutrition on immune function resonate with your personal wellness goals?

Understanding the profound connection between nutrition and immune health empowers you to make informed choices that can enhance your body's natural defenses and support overall well-being. In the upcoming chapters, we'll explore specific foods and dietary habits that can further boost your immune system and reduce the risk of illness.

Overview of the Book's Goals and Structure

As we embark on this journey through the fascinating world of nutrition and its impact on immune health, it's essential to understand the goals and structure of this book. By doing so, you'll gain a clear roadmap of what to expect and how to navigate the chapters ahead.

Setting the Goals

The primary goal of this book is to empower you with knowledge and practical insights into how nutrition can be a powerful tool in fortifying your immune system and reducing the risk of illness. We aim to achieve this through the following objectives:

Objective 1: Understand the Immune System

We'll delve deeper into the workings of your immune system, helping you grasp its intricacies and importance in protecting your body.

Objective 2: Explore the Impact of Nutrition

You'll discover how the nutrients you consume serve as the building blocks of your immune defenses, enhancing your understanding of the vital role of nutrition.

Objective 3: Discover Immune-Boosting Foods

We'll explore specific foods, dietary patterns, and culinary strategies that can optimize your immune health.

Objective 4: Provide Practical Guidance

This book is not just about theory; it's about practical application. You'll find actionable tips, meal plans, and recipes to help you incorporate immune-boosting foods into your daily life.

Objective 5: Promote Lifelong Wellness

Our ultimate goal is to inspire you to make sustainable changes in your dietary habits that support not only immediate immune health but also long-term well-being.

Navigating the Book's Structure

Now, let's take a quick tour of how this book is structured to achieve these goals:

Part I: Foundations of Immunity

In the initial sections of the book, we'll build a strong foundation of knowledge about the immune system and its intricate workings. You'll gain a deeper appreciation for how your body's defenses function and why nutrition is a crucial factor in this process.

Part II: Nutrients and Immune Health

In this section, we'll dive into the specific nutrients that play pivotal roles in immune health. From vitamins and minerals to proteins and phytonutrients, you'll learn how these components contribute to your body's immunity.

Part III: Immune-Boosting Foods

Here, we'll explore a wide range of foods that have been recognized for their immune-boosting properties. You'll discover how everyday choices in your diet can have a significant impact on your immune resilience.

Part IV: Practical Application

This part of the book is all about putting knowledge into action. You'll find practical guidance on meal planning, cooking, and making informed choices when it comes to nutrition and immune health.

Part V: Lifelong Wellness

Finally, we'll discuss the importance of maintaining a lifelong commitment to immune health. We'll explore strategies for sustaining healthy dietary habits and keeping your immune system robust throughout different stages of life.

Questions for Reflection:

1. What are your personal goals for reading this book? Are there specific aspects of immune health or nutrition you're particularly interested in?
2. How do you feel about the idea of making dietary changes to support your immune system? Are there any concerns or challenges you anticipate?
3. What role do you believe nutrition plays in achieving overall well-being and longevity?
4. As you look at the structure of this book, which sections or topics intrigue you the most?
5. How can you envision incorporating the knowledge and guidance from this book into your daily life for lasting immune health benefits?

As we progress through the chapters, keep these goals and the book's structure in mind. Our journey together is not only about learning but also about taking actionable steps toward a healthier, more resilient you.

The Importance of a Balanced Diet in Maintaining Overall Health

A balanced diet is the cornerstone of good health, and it forms the bedrock of a strong immune system. In this section, we'll delve into why maintaining a balanced diet is not just a dietary recommendation but a fundamental pillar of overall well-being.

Nourishing Your Body: A Holistic Approach

Imagine your body as a finely tuned instrument, and a balanced diet as the harmonious melody it produces. Just as a musical composition requires a delicate balance of notes and rhythms, your body relies on a diverse array of nutrients to function optimally.

Essential Nutrients: The Building Blocks of Health

A balanced diet provides your body with essential nutrients, including carbohydrates, proteins, fats, vitamins, and minerals. Each of these components plays a unique role in supporting your body's functions:

- **Carbohydrates:** They are the primary source of energy for your body, supplying the fuel needed for daily activities and immune responses.
- **Proteins:** Crucial for the repair and growth of tissues, including immune cells, proteins are like the builders of your body's defenses.
- **Fats:** Healthy fats are essential for cell membranes and are a source of energy. Omega-3 fatty acids, found in fatty fish and flaxseeds, have anti-inflammatory properties that support immune function.
- **Vitamins and Minerals:** These micronutrients act as cofactors for various biochemical reactions in your body, including those involved in immune responses. For example, vitamin C supports the production and function of immune cells, while zinc is essential for immune cell development and function.

Balancing Act: The Key to Health

A balanced diet is not about excluding specific food groups or adhering to rigid dietary restrictions. Instead, it's about achieving equilibrium by consuming a variety of foods from different food groups in the right proportions. This balance ensures that you receive all the essential nutrients your body needs to thrive.

The Immune Connection

Now, let's connect the dots between a balanced diet and immune health. When your body receives a consistent and adequate supply of essential nutrients, your immune system operates at its peak performance. Here's how it works:

- **Energy for Immunity:** Carbohydrates provide the energy necessary for immune cells to function effectively. Without sufficient energy, immune responses may be compromised.
- **Building Immune Defenses:** Proteins are essential for the production of antibodies, enzymes, and immune cells. They are the builders and repairers of your immune defenses.
- **Nutrient Support:** Vitamins and minerals, especially vitamins C, D, and E, and minerals like zinc, provide crucial support to immune cells. They enhance the immune system's ability to detect and neutralize pathogens.
- **Anti-Inflammatory Effects:** Healthy fats, such as those found in avocados, nuts, and olive oil, contribute to a well-balanced immune response. They help reduce chronic inflammation, which can weaken the immune system over time.

Questions for Reflection:

1. How would you describe your current dietary habits? Do you feel they align with the concept of a balanced diet?
2. Have you noticed any correlations between your diet and your overall health or susceptibility to illness?
3. Are there specific foods or food groups that you find challenging to incorporate into your diet? What strategies could help you include them?
4. How do you think maintaining a balanced diet might positively impact not only your immune health but also your overall well-

being?

5. What steps can you take to ensure that your daily meals align with the principles of a balanced diet?

Understanding the vital role of a balanced diet in supporting your immune system and overall health is the first step towards making informed dietary choices. As we progress through this book, you'll discover practical ways to incorporate these principles into your daily life, enhancing your well-being and immune resilience.

A Brief History of Research on Nutrition and Immunity

The study of nutrition and its impact on the immune system has a rich and fascinating history that spans centuries. As we embark on this journey into the intricate relationship between what we eat and how our bodies defend against pathogens, it's valuable to take a brief look back at the milestones in the history of this research.

Early Observations: The Discovery of Nutritional Deficiencies

The early roots of nutrition and immunity research can be traced back to the late 18th and early 19th centuries. During this period, scientists and explorers observed the profound effects of diet on health. For example, British naval surgeon James Lind conducted one of the earliest recorded clinical trials in 1747. His experiments with sailors suffering from scurvy demonstrated that citrus fruits, rich in vitamin C, could effectively prevent and cure the disease. This discovery marked the beginning of our understanding of the role of specific nutrients in maintaining health.

The Role of Vitamins: A Breakthrough in the Early 20th Century

The early 20th century witnessed significant breakthroughs in understanding the impact of vitamins on immunity. Researchers like Sir Frederick Hopkins and Casimir Funk made groundbreaking contributions by identifying essential nutrients such as vitamins and minerals. Hopkins, awarded the Nobel Prize in Physiology or Medicine in 1929, highlighted the critical role of vitamins in various physiological processes, including immune function.

World War II and Nutritional Research

World War II played a pivotal role in advancing nutrition and immunity research. The war necessitated the development of military rations that could sustain troops' health in challenging conditions. Nutritional scientists, alongside the military, worked on creating balanced diets for soldiers, highlighting the importance of adequate nutrition for immune resilience.

The Modern Era: Nutritional Immunology

In recent decades, the field of nutritional immunology has evolved significantly. Researchers have delved deeper into the complex interactions between specific nutrients, immune cells, and molecular pathways. Studies have illuminated the roles of vitamins, minerals, antioxidants, and phytonutrients in bolstering immune responses, reducing inflammation, and enhancing overall health.

Questions for Reflection:

1. How do you think the early observations and discoveries in nutrition and immunity research have shaped our understanding of diet and health today?
2. Can you think of any historical examples where nutrition played a crucial role in public health, especially during times of crisis or war?
3. In your opinion, why is it important to have a historical perspective on the study of nutrition and immunity?
4. How has your own awareness of nutrition and its impact on health evolved over time?
5. Are there specific areas of nutrition and immunity research that you find particularly intriguing and would like to learn more about?

By examining the historical milestones in nutrition and immunity research, we gain a deeper appreciation for the knowledge that informs our present understanding. This historical perspective underscores the significance of making informed dietary choices to support our immune health and overall well-being. As we delve deeper into this book, you'll discover how these historical insights continue to shape our approach to nutrition and immunity.

Chapter 2: The Basics of Immune-Boosting Nutrients

Key Vitamins and Minerals for Immune Health

When it comes to nourishing your immune system, certain vitamins and minerals stand out as essential players. Let's dive into these key nutrients and understand how they bolster your body's defenses.

Vitamin C: The Immune System's Guardian

Vitamin C, also known as ascorbic acid, is one of the most well-known immune-boosting vitamins. It plays a multifaceted role in supporting your immune system:

- **Antioxidant Power:** Vitamin C is a potent antioxidant, neutralizing free radicals that can damage immune cells. This antioxidant property helps maintain the integrity of your immune defenses.
- **Strengthening Immune Cells:** It promotes the production and function of various immune cells, including white blood cells, which are your body's frontline soldiers against pathogens.
- **Collagen Production:** Vitamin C is essential for collagen synthesis, a protein that helps repair and maintain the skin, mucous membranes, and other barriers that act as your body's first line of defense.

Vitamin D: The Sunshine Vitamin

Vitamin D is often referred to as the "sunshine vitamin" because your skin can produce it when exposed to sunlight. It has a profound impact on immune function:

- **Regulating Immune Responses:** Vitamin D helps modulate the immune system, preventing it from becoming overactive or underactive. This balance is crucial for effective immune responses.
- **Enhancing Antimicrobial Peptides:** It stimulates the production of antimicrobial peptides, which are natural antibiotics produced by your body to fight off infections.

- **Supporting Immune Cells:** Vitamin D supports the function of immune cells like macrophages and T-cells, which play critical roles in identifying and eliminating pathogens.

Vitamin E: The Immune System's Protector

Vitamin E is another essential antioxidant that contributes to immune health:

- **Neutralizing Free Radicals:** Like vitamin C, vitamin E protects immune cells from oxidative stress caused by free radicals. This preservation helps immune cells function optimally.
- **Enhancing Antibody Production:** Vitamin E supports the production of antibodies, which are proteins that specifically target and neutralize invaders.
- **Inhibiting Inflammation:** It can help reduce excessive inflammation, preventing it from impairing immune responses.

Zinc: The Immune System's Commander

Zinc is a crucial mineral that acts as a general of your immune system, coordinating and regulating various immune responses:

- **Immune Cell Function:** Zinc supports the development, activation, and function of immune cells, such as neutrophils and natural killer cells.
- **Antiviral Activity:** It may inhibit the replication of certain viruses, making it an important player in the battle against infections.
- **Wound Healing:** Zinc is essential for the healing of wounds and tissue repair, which are vital aspects of immune health.

Selenium: The Immune System's Protector

Selenium is a trace element that contributes to immune function:

- **Antioxidant Defense:** It acts as an antioxidant by supporting the function of enzymes that neutralize free radicals, protecting immune cells from damage.

- **Enhancing Immune Responses:** Selenium may enhance the production of antibodies and improve the function of immune cells.

Questions for Reflection:

1. How often do you consume foods rich in vitamin C, D, E, zinc, and selenium?
2. Are there specific dietary sources of these nutrients that you particularly enjoy?
3. Have you ever noticed changes in your health when you increased your intake of these immune-boosting nutrients?
4. Are there any dietary restrictions or preferences that may affect your ability to obtain these nutrients naturally?
5. How can you incorporate more foods rich in these vitamins and minerals into your daily meals?

These key vitamins and minerals serve as the foundation of your immune system's strength. By ensuring you have an adequate intake of these nutrients through a balanced diet, you equip your body with the tools it needs to defend against potential threats and maintain optimal immune health.

How Antioxidants Help Combat Free Radicals and Support Immunity

Antioxidants are the unsung heroes of your immune system. They play a pivotal role in safeguarding your health by combatting free radicals and bolstering your immunity. Let's unravel the remarkable partnership between antioxidants and your immune defenses.

Understanding Free Radicals: The Culprits of Oxidative Stress

Free radicals are highly reactive molecules that can cause oxidative stress in your body. They are generated as natural byproducts of cellular metabolism and play a role in immune responses. However, excessive free radicals can overwhelm your defenses and lead to cellular damage, inflammation, and increased susceptibility to illness.

Enter Antioxidants: The Immune Allies

Antioxidants are substances that neutralize free radicals, preventing them from causing harm. They work as immune allies by:

1. **Defending Immune Cells:** Antioxidants shield immune cells from oxidative stress, ensuring they remain fully functional and capable of responding to threats.
2. **Enhancing Immune Responses:** By reducing oxidative stress, antioxidants promote a balanced and effective immune response. Excessive oxidative stress can lead to immune dysfunction.
3. **Supporting Immune Cell Communication:** Antioxidants help maintain communication between immune cells, ensuring a coordinated response to infections.
4. **Reducing Inflammation:** Chronic inflammation can weaken the immune system. Antioxidants help mitigate inflammation, keeping the immune system in check.

Key Antioxidants for Immunity

Several antioxidants play crucial roles in supporting your immune system:

1. **Vitamin C:** As a potent antioxidant, vitamin C neutralizes free radicals, protects immune cells, and supports the production and function of immune cells.
2. **Vitamin E:** Vitamin E guards immune cells from oxidative damage and contributes to antibody production, strengthening immune responses.
3. **Selenium:** Selenium enhances the activity of antioxidant enzymes, defending immune cells from oxidative stress.
4. **Phytonutrients:** Found in colorful fruits and vegetables, phytonutrients like flavonoids and carotenoids have antioxidant properties that contribute to immune health.
5. **Zinc:** While not an antioxidant itself, zinc supports the function of antioxidant enzymes, indirectly assisting in oxidative stress defense.

Antioxidant-Rich Foods: Your Immune Arsenal

Incorporating antioxidant-rich foods into your diet is a powerful strategy to support your immune system:

- **Fruits and Vegetables:** Berries, citrus fruits, leafy greens, and colorful vegetables are abundant sources of antioxidants.
- **Nuts and Seeds:** Almonds, walnuts, and sunflower seeds are packed with vitamin E and other antioxidants.
- **Herbs and Spices:** Turmeric, ginger, and garlic contain phytonutrients with strong antioxidant properties.
- **Tea:** Green tea and black tea offer polyphenols, a type of antioxidant that may boost immunity.
- **Whole Grains:** Foods like oats and quinoa provide selenium, an essential antioxidant mineral.

Questions for Reflection:

1. Are you aware of the presence of antioxidants in your daily diet? What are your primary sources of antioxidants?
2. Have you ever experienced the benefits of an antioxidant-rich diet, such as improved immune resilience or reduced inflammation?
3. Are there any specific antioxidant-rich foods or recipes you enjoy incorporating into your meals?
4. How can you make conscious choices to include more antioxidants in your diet to support your immune health?
5. Have you considered the connection between antioxidants and your overall well-being, beyond just immune health?

Remember that antioxidants are not just supplements; they are abundant in natural foods. By embracing a diet rich in antioxidants, you empower your immune system to fend off threats and maintain your health and vitality. As we delve further into this book, you'll discover how to create delicious and nutrient-packed meals that are your immune system's best friend.

Sources of Immune-Boosting Nutrients in Common Foods

Your kitchen is a treasure trove of immune-boosting nutrients waiting to be discovered. Let's explore some everyday foods that are rich sources of vitamins, minerals, and antioxidants to support your immune health.

Vitamin C Sources

Vitamin C is a well-known immune-boosting nutrient, and you can find it in various foods:

- **Citrus Fruits:** Oranges, grapefruits, lemons, and limes are famous for their high vitamin C content. A glass of fresh orange juice or a citrus fruit salad can be a refreshing way to meet your daily vitamin C needs.
- **Strawberries:** These sweet and vibrant berries are not only delicious but also packed with vitamin C. Add them to your breakfast yogurt or enjoy them as a snack.
- **Bell Peppers:** Red, yellow, and green bell peppers are excellent sources of vitamin C. They can be incorporated into salads, stir-fries, or as crunchy snacks with hummus.
- **Broccoli:** This cruciferous vegetable is rich in vitamin C and other immune-boosting compounds. Steam, roast, or stir-fry broccoli to preserve its nutrients.

Vitamin D Sources

Vitamin D primarily comes from sunlight, but you can also obtain it from certain foods:

- **Fatty Fish:** Salmon, mackerel, and trout are among the best dietary sources of vitamin D. Grilled salmon or baked trout makes for a nutritious and immune-supportive meal.
- **Egg Yolks:** While the white of the egg contains proteins, the yolk is where you'll find vitamin D. Enjoy a sunny-side-up or poached egg to increase your intake.

- **Fortified Foods:** Some dairy products, orange juice, and cereals are fortified with vitamin D. Check the labels to find fortified options.

Vitamin E Sources

Vitamin E is readily available in a variety of foods:

- **Nuts and Seeds:** Almonds, sunflower seeds, and hazelnuts are rich in vitamin E. Sprinkle them on salads or enjoy them as a snack.
- **Spinach and Greens:** Leafy greens like spinach and Swiss chard contain vitamin E. Incorporate them into your salads, smoothies, or sautés.
- **Avocado:** Avocado is not only creamy and delicious but also a good source of vitamin E. Spread avocado on whole-grain toast or add it to salads and sandwiches.

Zinc Sources

Zinc is abundant in several foods:

- **Lean Meats:** Beef, pork, and poultry are excellent sources of zinc. Grill or roast lean cuts for a tasty and immune-supportive meal.
- **Legumes:** Beans, lentils, and chickpeas are plant-based sources of zinc. Create hearty soups, stews, or salads with these legumes.
- **Nuts:** Cashews, almonds, and peanuts contain zinc. Snacking on nuts or adding them to your dishes can boost your zinc intake.

Selenium Sources

Selenium can be found in various foods:

- **Fish:** Tuna, halibut, and sardines are seafood sources of selenium. Grill or bake fish for a nutrient-rich meal.
- **Brazil Nuts:** These nuts are exceptionally high in selenium. A small serving of Brazil nuts can provide your daily selenium requirement.
- **Whole Grains:** Brown rice, whole wheat bread, and oatmeal also

contain selenium. These grains can be incorporated into various meals.

Phytonutrient Sources

Phytonutrients are abundant in colorful fruits and vegetables:

- **Berries:** Blueberries, strawberries, and raspberries are rich in flavonoids, powerful antioxidants. Use them in smoothies, yogurt, or as toppings for oatmeal.
- **Tomatoes:** Tomatoes contain lycopene, a phytonutrient with antioxidant properties. Enjoy them in salads, soups, or as a pasta sauce.
- **Leafy Greens:** Kale, spinach, and collard greens are packed with phytonutrients like carotenoids. These greens can be used in salads, stir-fries, or smoothies.

Questions for Reflection:

1. Are there any immune-boosting foods mentioned above that you already incorporate into your diet?
2. Are there any new foods or recipes you'd like to try to increase your intake of these immune-boosting nutrients?
3. How do you currently plan your meals to ensure a variety of immune-boosting nutrients?
4. Have you noticed any changes in your health when you've increased your consumption of these nutrient-rich foods?
5. How can you make grocery shopping and meal planning more conducive to including these immune-boosting foods regularly?

Remember, your everyday meals can be a delicious way to fortify your immune system. By consciously choosing foods rich in these immune-boosting nutrients, you can support your body's defenses and enhance your overall well-being.

Recommended Daily Intake and Potential Deficiencies

Knowing how much of each immune-boosting nutrient you need and understanding the risk of deficiencies is crucial for maintaining optimal health. Let's explore the recommended daily intake and potential deficiencies of these vital nutrients.

Vitamin C: Recommended Daily Intake and Deficiency

- **Recommended Daily Intake:** The recommended daily intake of vitamin C varies by age and gender but typically falls in the range of 65 to 90 milligrams (mg) per day for adults. However, some experts suggest higher intake, especially during times of illness or stress.
- **Potential Deficiency:** Vitamin C deficiency can lead to scurvy, a condition characterized by fatigue, weakness, and swollen, bleeding gums. While severe deficiencies are rare in developed countries, suboptimal intake can weaken the immune system and increase susceptibility to infections.

Vitamin D: Recommended Daily Intake and Deficiency

- **Recommended Daily Intake:** The recommended daily intake of vitamin D also varies by age and gender. For adults, the general guideline is around 600 to 800 International Units (IU) per day. However, individual requirements can vary based on factors like sun exposure, age, and overall health.
- **Potential Deficiency:** Vitamin D deficiency is relatively common, particularly in regions with limited sunlight during certain seasons. A deficiency can result in weakened bones, impaired immune function, and an increased risk of infections.

Vitamin E: Recommended Daily Intake and Deficiency

- **Recommended Daily Intake:** The recommended daily intake of vitamin E for adults is typically around 15 milligrams (mg) per day.
- **Potential Deficiency:** Vitamin E deficiency is uncommon but can occur in individuals with specific medical conditions that hinder

nutrient absorption. Symptoms may include muscle weakness and vision problems. A deficiency can weaken immune function over time.

Zinc: Recommended Daily Intake and Deficiency

- **Recommended Daily Intake:** The recommended daily intake of zinc varies by age and gender. For adult men, it's around 11 mg per day, while for women, it's about 8 mg per day.
- **Potential Deficiency:** Zinc deficiency is more common in certain populations, such as vegetarians and vegans, as plant-based foods often contain compounds that inhibit zinc absorption. Deficiency can lead to impaired immune function, delayed wound healing, and increased susceptibility to infections.

Selenium: Recommended Daily Intake and Deficiency

- **Recommended Daily Intake:** The recommended daily intake of selenium is typically around 55 micrograms (mcg) for adults.
- **Potential Deficiency:** Selenium deficiency is uncommon in well-balanced diets. However, in regions with selenium-poor soils, deficiency can occur and may lead to muscle weakness and fatigue. A deficiency can also affect the immune system.

Phytonutrients: Recommended Daily Intake and Deficiency

Phytonutrients, being non-essential compounds, do not have specific recommended daily intakes. However, including a variety of colorful fruits and vegetables in your diet provides a broad spectrum of phytonutrients.

- **Potential Deficiency:** A diet lacking in diverse fruits and vegetables may result in lower phytonutrient intake, potentially diminishing the overall protective effect of these compounds on immune health.

Maintaining Optimal Nutrient Levels

To maintain optimal nutrient levels and minimize the risk of deficiencies, consider the following strategies:

1. **Balanced Diet:** Consume a well-balanced diet that includes a variety of nutrient-rich foods. This ensures you obtain essential vitamins, minerals, and antioxidants.
2. **Supplementation:** In cases where it's challenging to meet nutrient needs through diet alone, consider dietary supplements. However, it's essential to consult a healthcare professional before taking supplements, as excessive intake can be harmful.
3. **Regular Health Checkups:** Schedule regular health checkups to monitor your nutrient levels and address any deficiencies promptly.
4. **Sun Exposure:** Spend time outdoors to boost your vitamin D levels naturally through sunlight exposure, while being mindful of sun safety.

Questions for Reflection:

1. How confident are you in meeting your daily nutrient needs through your current diet?
2. Have you ever experienced symptoms that could be indicative of nutrient deficiencies, such as fatigue or weakened immunity?
3. Are there specific dietary choices or habits you could improve to enhance your nutrient intake and overall immune health?
4. Have you considered discussing nutrient supplementation with a healthcare professional, especially if you have specific health concerns or dietary restrictions?
5. How do you plan to maintain optimal nutrient levels to support your immune health in the long term?

Being mindful of your nutrient intake and understanding the recommended daily levels can help you proactively support your immune system and overall well-being. By making informed dietary choices and addressing potential deficiencies, you empower your body to function at its best, ready to defend against potential threats.

The Role of Water and Hydration in Immune System Function

When we think about immune health, we often focus on vitamins, minerals, and antioxidants. However, there's another essential player in this immune-boosting orchestra: water. Let's dive into the critical role of hydration in supporting your immune system.

The Foundation of Life: Water

Water is the foundation of life itself. Every cell, tissue, and organ in your body relies on water to function correctly. It's involved in numerous physiological processes, including those that contribute to a robust immune system:

1. **Lymphatic System Function:** The lymphatic system, a critical part of your immune system, relies on water to transport immune cells, nutrients, and waste products. Proper lymphatic circulation is vital for effective immune responses.
2. **Temperature Regulation:** Water helps regulate your body temperature. Maintaining a stable body temperature is essential for the optimal functioning of immune cells.
3. **Nutrient and Waste Transport:** Water carries nutrients to cells and removes waste products, ensuring that immune cells receive the energy and resources they need to operate efficiently.
4. **Mucous Membrane Maintenance:** Hydration supports the integrity of mucous membranes in your respiratory and gastrointestinal tracts. These membranes act as physical barriers against pathogens, preventing their entry into the body.

Dehydration and Immune Suppression

Conversely, inadequate hydration can lead to immune suppression and increased susceptibility to infections. Here's how dehydration can compromise your immune system:

1. **Reduced Immune Cell Function:** Dehydration can decrease the production and function of immune cells, impairing their ability to combat pathogens effectively.

2. **Altered Blood Viscosity:** When you're dehydrated, your blood becomes thicker, making it more challenging for immune cells to circulate throughout your body.
3. **Decreased Lymphatic Flow:** Insufficient hydration can slow lymphatic flow, hindering the transport of immune cells and molecules.
4. **Impaired Barrier Function:** Dehydration can lead to dry mucous membranes, making them less effective at trapping and neutralizing pathogens.

Maintaining Hydration for Immune Health

To support your immune system through hydration, consider the following tips:

1. **Daily Water Intake:** Aim to drink an adequate amount of water daily. The exact amount varies based on factors like age, sex, activity level, and climate but generally falls in the range of 2 to 3 liters (about 8 to 12 cups) per day.
2. **Monitor Hydration:** Pay attention to your body's signals of thirst. Feeling thirsty is a sign that you should drink water.
3. **Balanced Electrolytes:** In some situations, such as intense physical activity or hot weather, you may need to replenish electrolytes lost through sweating. Consider sports drinks or electrolyte-infused water.
4. **Diverse Fluid Sources:** While water is the primary source of hydration, you can also obtain fluids from fruits, vegetables, herbal teas, and soups.
5. **Consistent Hydration:** Maintain consistent hydration throughout the day, rather than relying on sporadic large amounts of water.

Questions for Reflection:

1. How mindful are you about staying hydrated throughout the day?
2. Do you tend to rely on water as your primary source of hydration, or

do you consume other hydrating beverages and foods?

3. Have you ever experienced the effects of dehydration, such as dry mouth or reduced energy levels?
4. Are there specific strategies you can implement to ensure you stay adequately hydrated, especially during busy or physically demanding periods?
5. How do you perceive the connection between hydration and immune health, and how can this awareness guide your daily habits?

Remember that maintaining proper hydration is not only essential for overall health but also plays a significant role in supporting your immune system. By making hydration a priority in your daily life, you provide your body with the necessary resources to mount a robust immune defense against potential threats.

Chapter 3: Gut Health and Immunity

The Gut Microbiome and Its Relationship to the Immune System

The gut microbiome, a bustling community of trillions of microorganisms residing in your digestive tract, plays a profound role in shaping your immune system. Let's embark on a journey to understand the intricate connection between these two essential components of your health.

The Gut Microbiome: A Diverse Ecosystem

Your gut is home to an incredibly diverse ecosystem of microorganisms, including bacteria, viruses, fungi, and other microbes. This thriving community, collectively known as the gut microbiome, exists in a delicate balance, contributing to various aspects of your well-being.

The Immune System's Surveillance

Your immune system is an ever-vigilant guardian, patrolling your body to detect and neutralize potential threats like viruses, bacteria, and toxins. However, it doesn't act alone; it relies on constant communication and interaction with the gut microbiome.

How Gut Microbes Influence Immune Responses

1. **Education of Immune Cells:** The gut microbiome helps educate immune cells, teaching them to differentiate between harmful invaders and beneficial microorganisms. This education is essential to prevent the immune system from attacking harmless substances.
2. **Immune Activation:** Gut microbes stimulate the immune system, promoting its readiness to respond to infections. They do this by producing molecules that alert immune cells to potential threats.
3. **Anti-Inflammatory Effects:** Some gut microbes produce anti-inflammatory compounds that help keep the immune system in check, preventing excessive inflammation that can harm healthy tissues.

4. **Barrier Maintenance:** A healthy gut microbiome contributes to the maintenance of the intestinal barrier. A strong barrier is crucial in preventing harmful pathogens from entering the bloodstream and triggering immune responses.

The Gut-Immune Connection in Action

Imagine your gut as the command center for immune responses. When a potential threat is detected in your digestive tract, the gut microbiome communicates with the immune system to coordinate a targeted response. This orchestrated effort ensures that your body can effectively defend itself against harmful invaders while tolerating the presence of beneficial microbes.

Nurturing a Healthy Gut Microbiome

To support your immune system through gut health, consider these strategies:

1. **Diverse Diet:** Consume a diverse range of fruits, vegetables, whole grains, and lean proteins. This diversity provides nourishment for a wide array of gut microbes.
2. **Fiber-Rich Foods:** Fiber serves as food for beneficial gut bacteria. Incorporate fiber-rich foods like beans, lentils, and whole grains into your meals.
3. **Probiotics:** Probiotic-rich foods like yogurt, kefir, and sauerkraut contain live beneficial bacteria that can enhance gut health.
4. **Prebiotics:** Prebiotics are non-digestible fibers that feed beneficial gut microbes. Foods like garlic, onions, and leeks are excellent sources of prebiotics.
5. **Hydration:** Proper hydration supports gut function and microbial balance.

Questions for Reflection:

1. How familiar are you with the concept of the gut microbiome and its influence on health?
2. Have you ever considered the connection between gut health and

immune function?

3. Are there specific dietary habits you practice that you think might be influencing your gut health?
4. How open are you to incorporating probiotic and prebiotic-rich foods into your diet to support your gut and immune health?
5. What steps can you take to nurture a healthy gut microbiome and, in turn, bolster your immune system?

Understanding the dynamic relationship between your gut microbiome and your immune system empowers you to make informed dietary choices that promote both digestive and immune health.

Prebiotics and Probiotics as Allies for a Healthy Gut

Nurturing a healthy gut is a key step in fortifying your immune system. Two essential players in this endeavor are prebiotics and probiotics. These dynamic duos work in harmony to create an optimal environment for your gut microbiome, ultimately supporting your overall well-being.

The Prebiotic Powerhouse

Prebiotics are non-digestible fibers found in certain foods. While your body can't break them down for energy, prebiotics serve as a feast for the beneficial bacteria in your gut. They promote the growth and activity of these friendly microbes, enhancing gut health and, in turn, supporting your immune system.

Sources of Prebiotics:

1. **Fruits:** Bananas, apples, and berries are rich in prebiotic fibers.
2. **Vegetables:** Garlic, onions, leeks, and asparagus are excellent sources.
3. **Whole Grains:** Foods like oats, barley, and whole wheat contain prebiotic fibers.
4. **Legumes:** Beans, lentils, and chickpeas are packed with prebiotics.

Probiotics: The Beneficial Bacteria

Probiotics are living microorganisms, often referred to as "good" or "friendly" bacteria, that provide numerous health benefits. These bacteria can be consumed through certain foods or supplements, and they directly influence the composition and balance of your gut microbiome.

Sources of Probiotics:

1. **Yogurt:** Yogurt contains live bacterial cultures, such as Lactobacillus and Bifidobacterium strains, known for their probiotic properties.
2. **Kefir:** This fermented dairy product is rich in beneficial bacteria and yeast strains.
3. **Sauerkraut:** Fermented cabbage is a source of Lactobacillus bacteria.
4. **Kimchi:** A spicy fermented cabbage dish from Korea, kimchi is teeming with probiotics.
5. **Fermented Pickles:** Naturally fermented pickles contain live cultures.
6. **Probiotic Supplements:** These are available in various forms, providing specific strains and concentrations of beneficial bacteria.

The Symbiotic Relationship

Prebiotics and probiotics complement each other, creating a symbiotic relationship that fosters gut health:

- **Prebiotics Feed Probiotics:** Prebiotics serve as nourishment for the probiotics in your gut, allowing them to thrive and exert their beneficial effects.
- **Enhanced Efficacy:** Consuming prebiotics alongside probiotics can enhance the survival and effectiveness of these beneficial microbes.
- **Balanced Gut Microbiome:** The combined action of prebiotics and probiotics promotes a balanced and diverse gut microbiome, which is essential for optimal immune function.

Questions for Reflection:

1. Are you familiar with prebiotics and probiotics, and have you ever

incorporated them into your diet?

2. Have you noticed any changes in your digestive health or overall well-being when consuming foods or supplements rich in prebiotics or probiotics?
3. Are there specific reasons or health goals that motivate you to consider adding more prebiotics and probiotics to your diet?
4. How open are you to exploring foods and recipes that incorporate these gut-boosting elements?
5. How do you envision the synergy between prebiotics and probiotics benefiting your gut health and immune system?

By integrating prebiotics and probiotics into your daily dietary choices, you can foster a flourishing gut microbiome that serves as a foundation for robust immune health.

How Fiber-Rich Foods Support Gut Health and Immunity

Fiber, often regarded as a humble component of our diet, holds a remarkable power when it comes to nurturing both gut health and immunity.

Understanding Dietary Fiber

Dietary fiber is a type of carbohydrate found in plant-based foods that our bodies cannot digest fully. Instead of being broken down and absorbed, it travels through the digestive tract largely intact, carrying out several crucial functions along the way.

Fiber's Role in Gut Health:

1. **Promoting Gut Microbiome Diversity:** Fiber serves as nourishment for beneficial gut bacteria, allowing them to flourish and maintain a balanced microbial community.
2. **Enhancing Bowel Regularity:** Insoluble fiber adds bulk to stool, aiding in the smooth passage of waste through the digestive tract, preventing constipation, and supporting gut health.
3. **Producing Short-Chain Fatty Acids:** Fermentable fibers are metabolized by gut bacteria to produce short-chain fatty acids

(SCFAs). SCFAs serve as an energy source for colon cells and contribute to a healthy gut lining.

4. **Reducing Inflammation:** A fiber-rich diet has been linked to lower levels of inflammation in the gut, which can help prevent chronic gut disorders.

Fiber's Immune-Boosting Potential:

1. **Supporting Gut-Immune Interaction:** A healthy gut lining, fostered by dietary fiber, aids in the proper interaction between gut-associated immune cells and the microbiome.
2. **Anti-Inflammatory Effects:** SCFAs produced from fiber fermentation have anti-inflammatory properties and may help regulate immune responses, preventing excessive inflammation.
3. **Enhancing Immune Cell Activity:** Some studies suggest that dietary fiber can enhance the activity of immune cells, such as T-cells, which play a crucial role in immune surveillance and defense.

Sources of Fiber-Rich Foods:

1. **Whole Grains:** Foods like oats, quinoa, brown rice, and whole wheat pasta are high in fiber.
2. **Legumes:** Beans, lentils, chickpeas, and peas are excellent sources of fiber.
3. **Fruits:** Berries, apples, pears, and citrus fruits are rich in soluble fiber.
4. **Vegetables:** Leafy greens, broccoli, carrots, and sweet potatoes contain a variety of fiber types.
5. **Nuts and Seeds:** Almonds, chia seeds, and flaxseeds are fiber-packed additions to your diet.

Practical Tips for Increasing Fiber Intake:

1. **Start Gradually:** If your current diet is low in fiber, introduce fiber-rich foods gradually to avoid digestive discomfort.
2. **Diverse Choices:** Incorporate a variety of fiber sources into your

meals to benefit from different types of fiber.

3. **Whole Foods:** Choose whole fruits, vegetables, and grains over processed options to maximize fiber content.
4. **Hydration:** Ensure you drink plenty of water when increasing fiber intake to aid in digestion.
5. **Balanced Meals:** Create balanced meals that include fiber-rich foods to support both gut health and immunity.

Questions for Reflection:

1. How conscious are you of your daily fiber intake, and do you actively seek out fiber-rich foods?
2. Have you ever experienced the digestive benefits of a high-fiber diet, such as improved regularity?
3. Are there specific foods or recipes that you enjoy incorporating into your meals to increase your fiber intake?
4. Have you noticed any changes in your overall well-being, particularly in terms of digestion and immune health, when you consume more fiber-rich foods?
5. How can you make fiber-rich foods a consistent and enjoyable part of your dietary habits?

Fiber-rich foods hold a dual role in supporting both your gut health and immune system. By embracing a diet abundant in these foods, you foster an environment in your body that not only promotes digestive wellness but also empowers your immune defenses to stand strong against potential threats. As we continue our exploration, you'll uncover practical strategies for weaving these foods into your daily meals, promoting vitality and resilience.

Linking Digestive Disorders to Compromised Immunity

Your digestive system is more than just a pathway for nutrients; it's a critical component of your immune system. Understanding the connection between digestive disorders and compromised immunity is essential for maintaining overall health and well-being.

The Digestive System: A Dual Role

Your digestive system serves two crucial functions:

1. **Nutrient Absorption:** It breaks down food, extracts nutrients, and delivers them to the bloodstream to nourish your body.
2. **Immune Defense:** It acts as a barrier to prevent harmful pathogens, toxins, and foreign substances from entering your body.

Digestive Disorders: Impact on Immunity

When digestive disorders disrupt the harmony of your digestive system, it can have profound consequences on your immune system:

1. **Leaky Gut Syndrome:** In conditions like leaky gut syndrome, the integrity of the intestinal lining is compromised, allowing undigested food particles and potentially harmful substances to enter the bloodstream. This can trigger an immune response and chronic inflammation, weakening overall immunity.
2. **Inflammatory Bowel Diseases (IBD):** Conditions like Crohn's disease and ulcerative colitis involve chronic inflammation of the digestive tract. This persistent inflammation can lead to immune system dysfunction and increased susceptibility to infections.
3. **Irritable Bowel Syndrome (IBS):** Although not an autoimmune condition, IBS can weaken the immune system indirectly by causing chronic stress and altering the gut microbiome, both of which impact immune function.
4. **Gastrointestinal Infections:** Infections like gastroenteritis can overwhelm the immune system and disrupt its balance. While the immune response is essential to clear the infection, chronic or severe cases can strain the immune system.
5. **Malnutrition:** Digestive disorders can impair nutrient absorption, leading to malnutrition. A deficiency in essential nutrients weakens the immune system's ability to function optimally.

Chronic Inflammation and Immunity

Chronic inflammation, a hallmark of many digestive disorders, can have far-reaching effects on the immune system:

1. **Immune System Exhaustion:** Constantly battling inflammation can wear out immune cells, making them less effective at defending against new threats.
2. **Imbalanced Immune Responses:** Chronic inflammation can lead to an imbalance in immune responses, potentially causing the immune system to overreact to harmless substances or underreact to dangerous invaders.
3. **Increased Susceptibility:** A compromised gut barrier, common in digestive disorders, can increase susceptibility to infections and other health issues.

Managing Digestive Disorders for Immune Health

To mitigate the impact of digestive disorders on immunity, consider the following strategies:

1. **Medical Management:** Work closely with healthcare professionals to manage and treat digestive disorders effectively.
2. **Dietary Choices:** Opt for foods that are easy on the digestive system during flare-ups. Incorporate anti-inflammatory foods like turmeric and ginger into your diet.
3. **Stress Reduction:** Chronic stress can exacerbate digestive disorders. Implement stress-management techniques like meditation and yoga.
4. **Probiotics and Prebiotics:** These can help restore gut balance and support both digestive and immune health.
5. **Nutritional Support:** If nutrient absorption is compromised, consider supplements or dietary modifications to address deficiencies.

Questions for Reflection:

1. Are you familiar with digestive disorders and their potential impact on the immune system?
2. Have you or someone you know experienced the link between

digestive issues and compromised immunity?

3. How proactive are you in seeking medical advice and treatment for digestive disorders when needed?

4. Are there specific dietary or lifestyle choices you can make to alleviate symptoms and support your immune system in the context of digestive disorders?

5. How do you perceive the connection between digestive health and overall well-being, and how can this awareness guide your choices?

Recognizing the connection between digestive disorders and compromised immunity underscores the importance of maintaining digestive health. By actively managing digestive issues and adopting a holistic approach to wellness, you can help your immune system operate at its full potential, safeguarding your health and vitality.

Tips for Maintaining a Balanced Gut Microbiome Through Diet

A balanced gut microbiome is the cornerstone of digestive health and a strong immune system. By making mindful dietary choices, you can nurture this essential ecosystem and promote overall well-being.

1. Embrace Dietary Diversity:

A diverse diet is key to a diverse microbiome. Consume a wide range of foods, including fruits, vegetables, whole grains, lean proteins, and plant-based options. Each type of food provides unique nutrients that support different gut bacteria.

2. Prioritize Fiber-Rich Foods:

Fiber is like a feast for your gut bacteria. It's found in plant-based foods like fruits, vegetables, legumes, and whole grains. Aim to include these fiber-rich foods in your daily meals to nourish beneficial gut microbes.

3. Include Fermented Foods:

Fermented foods are rich in probiotics, the friendly bacteria that support gut health. Incorporate yogurt, kefir, sauerkraut, kimchi, and other fermented foods into your diet. These foods can help populate your gut with beneficial microbes.

4. Opt for Prebiotics:

Prebiotics are non-digestible fibers that feed beneficial gut bacteria. Foods like garlic, onions, leeks, asparagus, and bananas are excellent sources of prebiotics. Include them in your meals to support the growth of beneficial microbes.

5. Limit Processed Foods:

Processed foods often lack the nutrients and fiber necessary to promote a healthy gut microbiome. They may also contain additives that can disrupt the balance of your gut bacteria. Minimize your intake of highly processed and sugary foods.

6. Experiment with Plant-Based Meals:

Plant-based diets rich in fruits, vegetables, and legumes can foster a diverse and balanced gut microbiome. Consider incorporating more vegetarian or vegan meals into your weekly menu.

7. Watch Your Sugar Intake:

Excessive sugar consumption can promote the growth of harmful bacteria in your gut. Limit your intake of sugary snacks, drinks, and desserts to maintain a balanced microbiome.

8. Stay Hydrated:

Proper hydration supports gut function and the transport of nutrients. Aim to drink enough water throughout the day to keep your digestive system running smoothly.

9. Be Mindful of Antibiotics:

While antibiotics are crucial for treating bacterial infections, they can also disrupt the balance of your gut microbiome. If prescribed antibiotics, follow your healthcare provider's guidance and consider probiotic supplements to help restore balance.

10. Manage Stress:

Chronic stress can affect your gut health. Practice stress-reduction techniques such as meditation, deep breathing, or yoga to support a healthy gut microbiome.

Questions for Reflection:

1. How diverse is your current diet in terms of fruits, vegetables, and whole grains?
2. Which fermented foods do you enjoy, and how often do you consume them?
3. Are you familiar with prebiotic-rich foods, and do you incorporate them into your meals?
4. Do you find it challenging to limit processed foods and sugary snacks in your diet?
5. Are there specific dietary changes you can make to promote a balanced gut microbiome and enhance your overall well-being?

Your dietary choices have a profound impact on your gut microbiome and, by extension, your immune system and overall health. By being mindful of the foods you consume and striving for a balanced diet rich in fiber and probiotic sources, you can create an environment within your body that supports optimal wellness and vitality.

Chapter 4: Inflammation and Immune Responses

Understanding Acute and Chronic Inflammation

Inflammation is a fundamental and complex aspect of the body's immune response. To fully comprehend its impact on your health, it's crucial to distinguish between acute and chronic inflammation, each with its unique characteristics and consequences.

Acute Inflammation: A Rapid Response

Acute inflammation is your body's immediate response to an injury, infection, or harmful substance. It's a short-lived, well-coordinated process that serves to protect and repair:

1. **Triggers:** Acute inflammation can be triggered by physical injuries, infections, burns, and irritants like splinters or pathogens.
2. **Key Players:** Immune cells, such as neutrophils and macrophages, rush to the site of injury or infection to neutralize threats.
3. **Symptoms:** Acute inflammation often results in classic symptoms like redness, heat, swelling, and pain. These symptoms are signs of increased blood flow and immune activity.
4. **Resolution:** Acute inflammation typically resolves once the threat is eliminated or the injury is repaired. This process includes anti-inflammatory mechanisms to restore tissue balance.

Chronic Inflammation: Prolonged Immune Activation

Chronic inflammation, on the other hand, is an ongoing, low-level inflammatory state that persists for an extended period. Unlike acute inflammation, it can be harmful:

1. **Causes:** Chronic inflammation can result from unresolved acute inflammation, autoimmune conditions, long-term exposure to irritants (e.g., smoking), or lifestyle factors like poor diet and chronic

stress.

2. **Duration:** Chronic inflammation can last for months or years, with cycles of flare-ups and remission.

3. **Impact:** Prolonged inflammation can damage tissues and organs, increasing the risk of chronic diseases such as heart disease, diabetes, and certain cancers.

4. **Subtle Symptoms:** Chronic inflammation often presents with subtle or nonspecific symptoms like fatigue, joint pain, or digestive issues. These symptoms may go unnoticed for an extended period.

Immune Responses in Inflammation: A Double-Edged Sword

In both acute and chronic inflammation, immune responses are at the core of the process. The immune system deploys various strategies to combat threats:

- **Immune Cells:** White blood cells, including lymphocytes, neutrophils, and macrophages, are mobilized to detect, neutralize, and remove harmful agents.
- **Cytokines:** These signaling molecules are released to coordinate immune responses and communicate with other cells.
- **Inflammation Mediators:** Pro-inflammatory and anti-inflammatory mediators help regulate the intensity and duration of inflammation.

Balancing Inflammation: The Yin and Yang of Immunity

While inflammation is essential for defending against infections and healing injuries, it must be carefully balanced. Overactive or chronic inflammation can harm healthy tissues and contribute to the development of chronic diseases.

Questions for Reflection:

1. Have you experienced acute inflammation, such as swelling from a sprained ankle or a fever during an infection? How did your body respond, and how quickly did the symptoms resolve?

2. Are you familiar with the concept of chronic inflammation, and do you know anyone who has dealt with chronic inflammatory

conditions?

3. Have you ever considered how lifestyle factors like diet, stress, or smoking can influence inflammation in your body?

4. How do you perceive the relationship between inflammation and immune responses, and how can this understanding guide your choices for a healthier life?

5. Are there specific symptoms or health concerns you've experienced that could be related to inflammation?

Recognizing the differences between acute and chronic inflammation empowers you to make informed choices to support a healthy immune response.

The Role of Anti-Inflammatory Foods in Immune Health

Inflammation is a double-edged sword, essential for defending the body against threats but potentially harmful when chronic or excessive. Thankfully, your diet can play a pivotal role in regulating inflammation and promoting immune health through anti-inflammatory foods.

Understanding Anti-Inflammatory Foods

Anti-inflammatory foods are those that possess properties to counteract or reduce inflammation in the body. They contain compounds that can help modulate the immune response and keep inflammation in check.

Key Anti-Inflammatory Compounds:

1. **Omega-3 Fatty Acids:** Found in fatty fish (e.g., salmon, mackerel), flaxseeds, chia seeds, and walnuts, omega-3s are renowned for their potent anti-inflammatory effects.

2. **Antioxidants:** Vitamins C and E, as well as various phytonutrients found in fruits and vegetables, combat oxidative stress and reduce inflammation.

3. **Polyphenols:** These plant compounds, present in foods like green tea, dark chocolate, berries, and red grapes, possess anti-inflammatory properties.

4. **Turmeric and Curcumin:** Turmeric, a spice commonly used in curries, contains curcumin, a powerful anti-inflammatory compound.
5. **Ginger:** Gingerol, found in ginger, has anti-inflammatory and antioxidant properties.

Supporting Immune Health with Anti-Inflammatory Foods

1. **Reducing Chronic Inflammation:** Chronic inflammation can weaken the immune system. Incorporating anti-inflammatory foods into your diet can help mitigate chronic inflammation and support a balanced immune response.
2. **Enhancing Antioxidant Defense:** Antioxidant-rich foods help protect immune cells from oxidative damage, ensuring they remain effective in fighting off infections.
3. **Regulating Immune Responses:** Certain anti-inflammatory compounds, like curcumin in turmeric, have been shown to modulate immune responses, preventing excessive inflammation.
4. **Supporting Gut Health:** Many anti-inflammatory foods, such as fiber-rich fruits and vegetables, promote gut health. A healthy gut is essential for a robust immune system.

Anti-Inflammatory Foods to Include:

1. **Fatty Fish:** Salmon, trout, sardines, and mackerel are excellent sources of omega-3 fatty acids.
2. **Berries:** Blueberries, strawberries, and raspberries are rich in antioxidants.
3. **Leafy Greens:** Spinach, kale, and Swiss chard provide a plethora of vitamins and antioxidants.
4. **Nuts and Seeds:** Almonds, walnuts, flaxseeds, and chia seeds are packed with healthy fats and antioxidants.
5. **Turmeric:** Incorporate turmeric into curries, soups, or smoothies for its anti-inflammatory benefits.
6. **Ginger:** Add fresh or powdered ginger to dishes, teas, or juices.

Practical Tips for an Anti-Inflammatory Diet:

1. **Balanced Meals:** Create balanced meals that include a variety of anti-inflammatory foods to support overall health.
2. **Hydration:** Stay well-hydrated with water, herbal teas, and hydrating foods like cucumbers and watermelon.
3. **Limit Processed Foods:** Minimize the intake of processed foods, as they often contain pro-inflammatory additives and unhealthy fats.
4. **Mindful Cooking:** Experiment with recipes that incorporate anti-inflammatory ingredients to make healthy eating enjoyable.
5. **Moderation:** While anti-inflammatory foods are beneficial, remember that overall dietary patterns matter. Strive for balance and moderation.

Questions for Reflection:

1. Are you familiar with the concept of anti-inflammatory foods, and do you incorporate them into your diet regularly?
2. Have you noticed any changes in your overall well-being, particularly in terms of energy levels or digestive health, when you consume more anti-inflammatory foods?
3. Are there specific foods or recipes you enjoy that contain anti-inflammatory ingredients?
4. How can you make anti-inflammatory foods a consistent and enjoyable part of your dietary habits to support your immune health?
5. How do you envision the connection between anti-inflammatory foods and immune health contributing to your overall well-being?

Integrating anti-inflammatory foods into your diet offers a proactive approach to managing inflammation and supporting immune health. As we continue our exploration, you'll uncover more strategies for harnessing the power of nutrition to optimize your body's immune responses and overall vitality.

Omega-3 Fatty Acids and Their Anti-Inflammatory Properties

Omega-3 fatty acids are unsung heroes in the realm of nutrition. These essential fats, primarily found in fatty fish, flaxseeds, chia seeds, and walnuts, wield potent anti-inflammatory properties that can significantly benefit your immune health and overall well-being.

Understanding Omega-3 Fatty Acids

Omega-3 fatty acids are a family of polyunsaturated fats with three primary members:

1. **ALA (Alpha-Linolenic Acid):** Found in plant-based sources like flaxseeds, chia seeds, and walnuts, ALA serves as a precursor for the other two omega-3s.
2. **EPA (Eicosapentaenoic Acid):** EPA is primarily found in fatty fish such as salmon, mackerel, and trout. It is renowned for its anti-inflammatory effects.
3. **DHA (Docosahexaenoic Acid):** Like EPA, DHA is found in fatty fish and is essential for brain health and development.

The Anti-Inflammatory Magic of Omega-3s

Omega-3 fatty acids are known for their ability to combat inflammation and support immune health:

1. **Reducing Pro-Inflammatory Molecules:** Omega-3s can help decrease the production of pro-inflammatory molecules in the body, thus dampening the inflammatory response.
2. **Promoting Anti-Inflammatory Molecules:** They also stimulate the production of anti-inflammatory molecules, creating a balanced and less aggressive immune response.
3. **Resolving Inflammation:** Omega-3s play a role in resolving inflammation by encouraging the body to produce specialized pro-resolving mediators (SPMs) that help bring the inflammatory process to a close.
4. **Immune Cell Function:** These fatty acids can enhance the function of immune cells, making them more efficient at combating infections

and illnesses.

Sources of Omega-3 Fatty Acids:

1. **Fatty Fish:** Salmon, mackerel, trout, sardines, and herring are some of the best sources of EPA and DHA.
2. **Plant-Based Sources:** Flaxseeds, chia seeds, walnuts, hemp seeds, and algae-based supplements are rich in ALA.

Incorporating Omega-3s into Your Diet:

1. **Fatty Fish:** Aim to include fatty fish in your diet at least twice a week to meet your EPA and DHA needs.
2. **Plant-Based Options:** If you follow a vegetarian or vegan diet, incorporate ALA-rich sources into your meals regularly. Consider flaxseed oil, chia seeds, and walnuts.
3. **Supplements:** Omega-3 supplements, such as fish oil capsules or algae-based supplements, can be beneficial if it's challenging to obtain sufficient omega-3s from food alone. Consult a healthcare professional before adding supplements to your routine.

Questions for Reflection:

1. Are you familiar with omega-3 fatty acids and their potential benefits for immune health?
2. Have you ever consciously included omega-3-rich foods in your diet, such as fatty fish or plant-based sources like flaxseeds or chia seeds?
3. Have you noticed any changes in your overall well-being when consuming omega-3-rich foods?
4. How open are you to incorporating more omega-3s into your diet through dietary choices or supplements to support your immune health?
5. How do you envision the anti-inflammatory properties of omega-3s contributing to your overall vitality and resilience?

Omega-3 fatty acids, with their remarkable anti-inflammatory properties, are a gift from nature to support your immune system and overall health.

Foods That May Exacerbate Inflammation and Weaken Immunity

While we've discussed the power of anti-inflammatory foods, it's equally important to recognize that certain dietary choices can fan the flames of inflammation and compromise your immune health. By understanding these foods, you can make informed decisions to support a balanced immune response.

1. Sugar and Refined Carbohydrates:

- **The Problem:** Foods high in added sugars and refined carbohydrates, such as sugary snacks, sweetened beverages, and white bread, can lead to rapid spikes in blood sugar levels. This can trigger inflammation and weaken immune cells' function.
- **Impact on Immunity:** Excessive sugar consumption can impair the ability of white blood cells to combat infections. It may also contribute to chronic inflammation, increasing the risk of chronic diseases.

2. Trans Fats:

- **The Problem:** Trans fats, often found in partially hydrogenated oils and many processed and fried foods, are pro-inflammatory. They promote inflammation by increasing the production of inflammatory markers in the body.
- **Impact on Immunity:** Trans fats can hinder the proper functioning of immune cells, making the body less effective at defending against infections.

3. Highly Processed Foods:

- **The Problem:** Highly processed foods, including fast food, frozen meals, and many packaged snacks, are often laden with additives, preservatives, and artificial flavors. These can trigger inflammatory responses in the body.

- **Impact on Immunity:** Chronic consumption of processed foods can contribute to chronic inflammation, weakening the immune system over time.

4. Saturated and Trans Fats:

- **The Problem:** Saturated fats, found in red meat, full-fat dairy products, and certain oils like palm and coconut oil, can promote inflammation when consumed in excess. They also raise LDL ("bad") cholesterol levels, which can have negative effects on immunity.
- **Impact on Immunity:** Diets high in saturated and trans fats can impair immune cell function and create an inflammatory environment in the body.

5. Excessive Alcohol:

- **The Problem:** Chronic alcohol consumption can lead to liver inflammation and weaken the immune system. It can also disrupt the balance of gut bacteria, affecting overall immune health.
- **Impact on Immunity:** The immune system relies on a healthy liver to detoxify the body. Excessive alcohol consumption can impair this process and compromise immune function.

6. Excessive Salt:

- **The Problem:** High-sodium diets, often associated with processed and restaurant foods, can lead to high blood pressure and inflammation.
- **Impact on Immunity:** Elevated blood pressure and inflammation can strain the cardiovascular system, potentially affecting immune responses.

7. Food Allergens:

- **The Problem:** Food allergies and sensitivities can trigger immune responses in the body. For individuals with these conditions, consuming allergenic foods can lead to chronic inflammation.
- **Impact on Immunity:** Chronic inflammation caused by food allergies can weaken the immune system and increase susceptibility to infections.

Questions for Reflection:

1. Are you aware of the potential impact of certain foods on inflammation and immune health?
2. Do you recognize any dietary habits that involve the consumption of foods high in sugar, trans fats, or excessive salt?
3. Have you ever experienced adverse reactions to specific foods or noticed changes in your overall well-being related to your diet?
4. How open are you to making dietary adjustments to reduce inflammation and support your immune system's strength and resilience?
5. How do you envision a more balanced and inflammation-reducing diet contributing to your overall health and vitality?

Being mindful of foods that can exacerbate inflammation and weaken immunity is a proactive step in nurturing your body's defense mechanisms.

Strategies for Adopting an Anti-Inflammatory Diet

Embracing an anti-inflammatory diet can be a transformative step in supporting your immune health and overall well-being. Here are practical strategies to help you make this important dietary shift.

1. Focus on Whole Foods:

- **The Power of Plants:** Base your diet on a variety of whole plant foods like fruits, vegetables, legumes, and whole grains. These foods are rich in vitamins, minerals, antioxidants, and fiber, all of which combat inflammation.

- **Lean Proteins:** Choose lean sources of protein, such as poultry, fish, tofu, and legumes. These options provide essential amino acids without the saturated fats found in red meat.

2. Opt for Healthy Fats:

- **Omega-3 Rich Foods:** Incorporate fatty fish like salmon and mackerel into your diet for their omega-3 fatty acids. For plant-based sources, include flaxseeds, chia seeds, and walnuts.
- **Healthy Oils:** Use heart-healthy oils like olive oil, which contains monounsaturated fats and antioxidants, to replace saturated and trans fats in cooking.

3. Reduce Sugar and Refined Carbohydrates:

- **Limit Added Sugars:** Minimize sugary snacks, sugary beverages, and processed foods high in added sugars. Opt for naturally sweet foods like fruits.
- **Choose Whole Grains:** Replace refined carbohydrates like white bread with whole grains like whole wheat, quinoa, and brown rice for sustained energy and lower inflammation.

4. Embrace Anti-Inflammatory Spices:

- **Turmeric:** Incorporate turmeric into your cooking. Curcumin, the active compound in turmeric, has potent anti-inflammatory properties.
- **Ginger:** Use fresh or powdered ginger in recipes, teas, and smoothies to harness its anti-inflammatory benefits.

5. Prioritize Plant-Based Proteins:

- **Legumes:** Beans, lentils, chickpeas, and tofu are excellent sources of plant-based protein. They also provide fiber, vitamins, and minerals that support an anti-inflammatory diet.

6. Include Colorful Antioxidant-Rich Foods:

- **Variety of Fruits and Vegetables:** Consume a rainbow of fruits and vegetables. The different colors indicate a variety of phytonutrients that combat inflammation.

7. Moderate Dairy and Red Meat:

- **Consider Alternatives:** If you consume dairy, opt for low-fat or plant-based alternatives. Limit red meat consumption and choose lean cuts when you do indulge.

8. Hydration and Herbal Teas:

- **Water:** Stay well-hydrated with water, which supports all bodily functions, including immune health.
- **Herbal Teas:** Enjoy herbal teas like green tea, which contains antioxidants that combat inflammation.

9. Plan Balanced Meals:

- **Balanced Plate:** Aim for balanced meals that include a source of lean protein, whole grains, and plenty of vegetables.

10. Mindful Eating:

- **Portion Control:** Be mindful of portion sizes to prevent overeating, which can contribute to inflammation.
- **Slow Eating:** Slow down during meals, savoring each bite and paying attention to hunger and fullness cues.

11. Cooking Techniques:

- **Baking and Grilling:** Opt for baking, grilling, or steaming over frying, which can add unhealthy fats to your diet.

12. Limit Processed Foods:

- **Read Labels:** Check food labels for hidden sources of added sugars, unhealthy fats, and artificial additives.

13. Stay Informed:

- **Continual Learning:** Stay informed about the latest research on nutrition and inflammation to make informed dietary choices.

Questions for Reflection:

1. How open are you to making dietary changes to adopt an anti-inflammatory diet?
2. Which of the suggested strategies align with your current dietary habits, and which ones do you find most challenging?
3. Have you experienced the benefits of an anti-inflammatory diet, such as increased energy or improved well-being?
4. Are there specific recipes or meal ideas you'd like to explore to incorporate more anti-inflammatory foods into your diet?
5. How do you envision embracing an anti-inflammatory diet contributing to your overall health and vitality?

Adopting an anti-inflammatory diet is a powerful step toward enhancing your immune health and promoting overall well-being.

Chapter 5: Building a Strong Immune Foundation in Childhood

The Critical Role of Nutrition in Children's Immune Development

Childhood is a time of rapid growth and development, and nutrition plays a pivotal role in shaping a strong immune foundation for the future.

Immune Development in Childhood

Children are born with an immature immune system that matures gradually over the early years of life. Proper immune development during childhood sets the stage for a robust and responsive immune system throughout adulthood.

Nutrition as the Building Blocks:

1. **Essential Nutrients:** Nutrients like vitamins (e.g., A, C, D, E) and minerals (e.g., zinc, iron) are essential for immune cell development and function. Adequate intake of these nutrients is crucial for a child's immune system to function optimally.
2. **Protein:** Protein is necessary for the production of antibodies, which are proteins that play a key role in the immune response.
3. **Omega-3 Fatty Acids:** Omega-3 fatty acids found in fatty fish, flaxseeds, and walnuts support the development of immune cells and help regulate inflammation.

The Role of Breastfeeding:

1. **Colostrum:** Breast milk, particularly colostrum, is rich in antibodies and immune-boosting compounds. It provides newborns with essential immune protection during their first days of life.
2. **Ongoing Immune Support:** Breastfeeding continues to support a child's immune system throughout infancy and early childhood by providing a wide range of nutrients and immune factors.

Diverse Diet, Stronger Immunity:

1. **Introducing Solid Foods:** As children transition to solid foods, introducing a variety of fruits, vegetables, whole grains, and lean proteins ensures they receive a broad spectrum of nutrients that support immune development.
2. **Fruits and Vegetables:** The vitamins, minerals, and antioxidants in fruits and vegetables strengthen the immune system. Encouraging children to enjoy a rainbow of colorful produce is an excellent way to bolster their defenses.

Maintaining a Balanced Diet:

1. **Limiting Processed Foods:** Processed foods high in added sugars and unhealthy fats should be limited. These foods can lead to inflammation and undermine immune health.
2. **Hydration:** Staying hydrated is essential for overall health, including immune function. Encourage children to drink water and consume hydrating foods like watermelon and cucumber.

Nutritional Supplements:

1. **Consult a Pediatrician:** In some cases, pediatricians may recommend nutritional supplements like vitamin D or iron to address specific deficiencies that could compromise immune health.

A Supportive Environment:

1. **Emotional Health:** A child's emotional well-being also influences immune health. A loving and nurturing environment contributes to a strong immune foundation.

Questions for Reflection:

1. Are you aware of the critical role of nutrition in children's immune development?
2. If you have children, do you consider their dietary choices and overall nutrition in the context of their immune health?

3. Have you noticed any correlations between your child's dietary habits and their overall well-being or susceptibility to illnesses?
4. How do you envision the long-term impact of providing proper nutrition for your child's immune development?
5. Are there specific dietary changes or habits you can implement to better support your child's immune foundation?

Nurturing a child's immune development through nutrition is a gift that keeps on giving, laying the groundwork for a lifetime of resilient health.

Breastfeeding and Its Immune-Boosting Benefits

Breastfeeding is a natural wonder that provides a multitude of immune-boosting benefits to infants

Colostrum: Liquid Gold for Immunity

1. **First Milk:** Colostrum, often referred to as "liquid gold," is the first milk produced by a mother's breasts during the initial days after birth. It is exceptionally rich in immune-boosting compounds.
2. **Antibodies:** Colostrum is packed with antibodies, also known as immunoglobulins, which provide passive immunity to the newborn. These antibodies protect against various infections and illnesses.
3. **Immune Factors:** Colostrum contains numerous immune factors such as lactoferrin, lysozyme, and white blood cells that enhance the infant's immune response.

Continual Immune Support:

1. **Ongoing Benefits:** Breast milk continues to provide immune support throughout infancy and early childhood. It adapts to the changing needs of the growing infant.
2. **Nutrient Density:** Breast milk is nutritionally dense, supplying essential vitamins, minerals, and proteins that support immune cell development and function.
3. **Digestibility:** Breast milk is easily digestible, reducing the risk of

gastrointestinal infections in infants.

Protection Against Infections:

1. **Reduced Risk:** Breastfed infants have a lower risk of respiratory infections, ear infections, gastrointestinal infections, and urinary tract infections.
2. **Allergies and Autoimmune Conditions:** Breastfeeding may reduce the risk of allergies, asthma, and autoimmune conditions in children.

Enhanced Gut Health:

1. **Gut Microbiome:** Breast milk promotes the development of a healthy gut microbiome. A balanced gut microbiome is essential for a strong immune system.
2. **Prebiotics:** Breast milk contains prebiotics that nourish beneficial gut bacteria, fostering a balanced and resilient microbiome.

Emotional Bond and Comfort:

1. **Emotional Well-Being:** Beyond its physical benefits, breastfeeding fosters a strong emotional bond between mother and child, contributing to the child's overall well-being.
2. **Comfort:** Breastfeeding provides comfort and a sense of security to infants, which can help reduce stress and positively impact the immune system.

Questions for Reflection:

1. Are you familiar with the numerous immune-boosting benefits of breastfeeding for infants?
2. If you are a parent or caregiver, did you choose to breastfeed your child, and if so, were you aware of its immune-boosting advantages?
3. Have you noticed any differences in the health and well-being of breastfed infants compared to those who were not breastfed?
4. How do you perceive the emotional and physical connection

between breastfeeding and an infant's immune health?

5. If you are considering breastfeeding or providing support to a breastfeeding mother, how do you envision its impact on the child's immune foundation?

Breastfeeding is not only a beautiful expression of maternal care but also a powerful tool in building a strong immune foundation for children.

Introducing Solid Foods and Creating a Balanced Diet for Kids

As children grow, their nutritional needs evolve, and introducing solid foods plays a vital role in nurturing their immune health

The Transition to Solids:

1. **Timing:** Pediatricians typically recommend introducing solid foods around 6 months of age. At this point, infants have developed the motor skills needed for eating and are ready to expand their diet beyond breast milk or formula.
2. **First Foods:** Start with single-ingredient, easy-to-digest foods like rice cereal, pureed fruits, or vegetables. Gradually introduce new foods one at a time to monitor for allergies.

The Building Blocks of a Balanced Diet:

1. **Fruits and Vegetables:** Offer a variety of colorful fruits and vegetables. These provide essential vitamins, minerals, antioxidants, and fiber that support immune function. Encourage children to try new fruits and vegetables to expand their palate.
2. **Protein:** Lean protein sources like poultry, fish, beans, lentils, and tofu are crucial for the growth and development of immune cells.
3. **Whole Grains:** Whole grains like whole wheat bread, brown rice, and oats provide complex carbohydrates and fiber, offering sustained energy and supporting overall health.
4. **Dairy or Dairy Alternatives:** Choose low-fat or fat-free dairy products, or opt for dairy alternatives like fortified almond or soy

milk. Dairy provides calcium and vitamin D, which are essential for bone health and immune function.

5. **Healthy Fats:** Incorporate healthy fats like avocados, nuts, and olive oil. These fats provide essential fatty acids that contribute to immune cell development.

Balancing Macronutrients:

1. **Protein:** Ensure children receive an adequate amount of protein for their growth and development. Protein is essential for building antibodies and immune cells.
2. **Carbohydrates:** Complex carbohydrates from fruits, vegetables, and whole grains provide energy and fiber to support overall health and immune function.
3. **Fats:** Include sources of healthy fats like avocados, nuts, and seeds. These fats are vital for the absorption of fat-soluble vitamins (A, D, E, K) important for immune health.

Hydration:

1. **Water:** Encourage children to drink water throughout the day to stay well-hydrated. Proper hydration is essential for overall health and immune function.

Snacking Wisely:

1. **Nutrient-Rich Snacks:** Provide nutrient-rich snacks like yogurt, cut-up fruits, or whole-grain crackers with cheese. These snacks support immune health and provide energy between meals.

Limiting Processed Foods:

1. **Minimize Sugary and Processed Snacks:** Limit the intake of sugary snacks, sugary beverages, and highly processed foods. These items can contribute to inflammation and weaken the immune system.

Supplements:

1. **Consult a Pediatrician:** In certain cases, pediatricians may recommend specific supplements to address nutritional deficiencies or unique dietary needs.

Questions for Reflection:

1. If you are a parent or caregiver, how did you approach introducing solid foods to your child, and what have you observed about their dietary preferences?
2. Are you familiar with the key components of a balanced diet for children that support their immune health and overall well-being?
3. Have you noticed any correlations between your child's dietary habits and their overall health or susceptibility to illnesses?
4. How open are you to making dietary adjustments to ensure your child receives a balanced and immune-supportive diet?
5. How do you envision the long-term impact of providing a balanced diet for your child's immune development and overall vitality?

Introducing solid foods and cultivating a balanced diet for children is a vital step in fortifying their immune foundation.

Food Allergies and Sensitivities in Relation to Childhood Immunity

Food allergies and sensitivities can have a profound impact on childhood immunity.

Understanding Food Allergies and Sensitivities:

1. **Food Allergies:** Food allergies are immune system reactions triggered by specific proteins in foods. The immune system mistakenly identifies these proteins as harmful invaders, leading to an allergic response. Common allergenic foods include peanuts, tree nuts, dairy, eggs, soy, wheat, fish, and shellfish.
2. **Food Sensitivities:** Food sensitivities, on the other hand, do not

involve the immune system's immediate allergic response. Instead, they often manifest as digestive discomfort or other symptoms after consuming certain foods. Common sensitivities include lactose intolerance and non-celiac gluten sensitivity.

The Impact on Immune Health:

1. **Allergies and Immune Activation:** Food allergies can result in the immune system's overactivation, leading to symptoms such as hives, swelling, digestive distress, or even anaphylaxis in severe cases.
2. **Inflammation:** Both food allergies and sensitivities can trigger inflammation in the body. Chronic inflammation can compromise the immune system's ability to defend against infections.
3. **Gut Health:** Food allergies and sensitivities can affect gut health, as they often involve reactions in the digestive system. A healthy gut is essential for a robust immune system.

Managing Food Allergies and Sensitivities:

1. **Consult a Healthcare Professional:** If you suspect your child has a food allergy or sensitivity, consult a healthcare professional for testing and diagnosis. This is crucial for proper management.
2. **Allergen Avoidance:** For diagnosed food allergies, strict allergen avoidance is the primary management strategy. Clear communication with caregivers and schools is essential to prevent accidental exposure.
3. **Dietary Modifications:** In the case of food sensitivities, dietary modifications may be recommended. For example, individuals with lactose intolerance can opt for lactose-free dairy or dairy alternatives.
4. **Gut Health:** Supporting gut health through a balanced diet that includes fiber-rich foods and probiotics can help mitigate the impact of food sensitivities on the digestive system.
5. **Consultation with an Allergist:** An allergist can provide guidance on potential treatments, such as allergen-specific immunotherapy (desensitization), for certain allergies.

Emotional Support:

1. **Psychological Impact:** Living with food allergies or sensitivities can have a psychological impact on children and their families. Emotional support and education are crucial for coping and managing these conditions effectively.

Questions for Reflection:

1. Are you familiar with the distinction between food allergies and sensitivities and their potential impact on childhood immunity?
2. Do you or someone you know have a child with food allergies or sensitivities? How has this condition influenced their dietary choices and overall well-being?
3. Have you observed any correlations between the management of food allergies or sensitivities and the child's overall health and susceptibility to illnesses?
4. How open are you to seeking professional guidance and making necessary dietary modifications if you suspect or are diagnosed with food allergies or sensitivities in your child?
5. How do you envision providing emotional support and education to children with food allergies or sensitivities, ensuring they have a positive relationship with food and their immune health?

Navigating food allergies and sensitivities in childhood requires diligence, education, and support to ensure the child's immune foundation remains strong.

Teaching Healthy Eating Habits to Children for Lifelong Wellness

One of the greatest gifts we can give our children is the knowledge and practice of healthy eating habits.

The Formative Years:

1. **Establishing Habits:** Childhood is a critical period for establishing

lifelong habits, including those related to nutrition. Habits formed in these early years often persist into adulthood.

2. **Dietary Preferences:** Early exposure to a variety of foods can shape children's taste preferences and willingness to try new foods. This diversity contributes to a balanced diet.

The Link Between Nutrition and Immune Health:

1. **Building a Strong Foundation:** Proper nutrition is fundamental for immune development. A balanced diet provides essential nutrients, vitamins, and minerals that support immune cell function.

2. **Resilience to Infections:** Children with healthy eating habits may experience fewer infections and illnesses due to their strengthened immune systems.

Strategies for Teaching Healthy Eating Habits:

1. **Be a Role Model:** Children often emulate the eating habits of their parents and caregivers. Set a positive example by enjoying a balanced diet yourself.

2. **Family Meals:** Aim to have regular family meals together. This fosters a sense of community and encourages healthier food choices.

3. **Involve Children:** Involve children in meal planning, grocery shopping, and cooking. When children have a hand in preparing their meals, they are more likely to be open to trying new foods.

4. **Food Education:** Educate children about the importance of various food groups, the nutrients they provide, and how they support overall health. Make learning about nutrition fun and engaging.

5. **Limit Processed Foods:** Minimize the consumption of processed and sugary foods. Instead, emphasize whole, nutrient-dense options.

6. **Balanced Meals:** Encourage balanced meals that include a source of protein, whole grains, and a variety of colorful fruits and vegetables.

7. **Hydration:** Teach the importance of staying hydrated by drinking water throughout the day. Limit sugary beverages.

8. **Moderation:** Teach children about portion control and moderation.

Allowing occasional treats is okay, as long as they are part of an overall balanced diet.

9. **Positive Reinforcement:** Praise and positively reinforce healthy eating choices. Avoid using food as a reward or punishment.

Addressing Picky Eating:

1. **Patience:** It's common for children to be selective about their food choices. Be patient and avoid pressuring them to eat certain foods.
2. **Variety:** Offer a variety of foods, and don't be discouraged if a child initially rejects something. It may take several exposures before they develop a taste for it.

Questions for Reflection:

1. Are you aware of the long-lasting impact of teaching healthy eating habits to children during their formative years?
2. If you have children or interact with them regularly, how do you currently approach teaching them about nutrition and healthy eating habits?
3. Have you observed any changes in a child's behavior or overall well-being as a result of positive dietary influences?
4. How open are you to implementing strategies for teaching healthy eating habits to children, whether in your family or community?
5. How do you envision the lifelong benefits of these habits, including strong immune health, positively shaping the lives of children?

Teaching healthy eating habits to children is an investment in their lifelong wellness, including the resilience and strength of their immune systems.

Chapter 6: Immune-Boosting Diets and Eating Patterns

Exploring Dietary Approaches: Mediterranean Diet and Plant-Based Diets

Dietary approaches play a pivotal role in boosting the immune system and promoting overall well-being.

The Mediterranean Diet: A Taste of the Mediterranean

1. **Overview:** The Mediterranean diet is inspired by the traditional eating patterns of countries bordering the Mediterranean Sea. It emphasizes whole, unprocessed foods and healthy fats.
2. **Key Components:**

- **Fruits and Vegetables:** Abundant intake of colorful fruits and vegetables provides vitamins, minerals, and antioxidants that support immune function.
- **Olive Oil:** Rich in monounsaturated fats and antioxidants, olive oil contributes to a balanced diet and helps reduce inflammation.
- **Whole Grains:** Whole grains like brown rice, whole wheat bread, and quinoa offer fiber, vitamins, and minerals that bolster overall health.
- **Lean Proteins:** Fish, poultry, legumes, and nuts provide protein without the saturated fats found in red meat.
- **Moderate Wine Consumption:** In moderation, red wine may offer antioxidants and anti-inflammatory benefits.

Plant-Based Diets: The Power of Plants

1. **Overview:** Plant-based diets, which include vegetarian and vegan approaches, prioritize plant foods while minimizing or eliminating animal products.
2. **Key Components:**

- **Abundance of Plants:** Fruits, vegetables, legumes, nuts, seeds, and whole grains make up the majority of plant-based diets. These foods are rich in nutrients and antioxidants that support immune health.
- **Low in Saturated Fat:** Plant-based diets tend to be low in saturated fat, which can reduce inflammation and promote heart health.
- **Fiber-Rich:** High fiber content supports digestive health and a balanced gut microbiome, essential for a strong immune system.
- **Omega-3 Sources:** Include sources like flaxseeds, chia seeds, walnuts, and algae-based supplements to ensure an adequate intake of omega-3 fatty acids.
- **Variety:** The variety of plant foods in these diets provides a wide array of nutrients and phytonutrients that promote immune resilience.

Benefits for Immune Health:

1. **Reduced Inflammation:** Both the Mediterranean diet and plant-based diets have been associated with reduced inflammation in the body, which can enhance immune function.
2. **Antioxidant-Rich:** These diets are rich in antioxidants that protect cells from damage and help maintain a strong immune system.
3. **Gut Health:** The abundance of fiber and plant foods in these diets supports a healthy gut microbiome, crucial for immune responses.
4. **Balanced Fat Intake:** Healthy fats, such as those found in olive oil and plant-based sources, are beneficial for overall health and immune function.

Questions for Reflection:

1. Are you familiar with the Mediterranean diet and plant-based diets and their potential benefits for immune health?
2. Have you considered adopting elements of these dietary approaches into your own eating patterns to boost your immune health?
3. How open are you to exploring new foods and recipes inspired by these diets?

4. Can you envision the long-term impact of incorporating elements of these diets on your overall well-being, including a stronger immune system?

5. Are there specific foods or meal ideas from these dietary approaches that you find particularly appealing or intriguing?

Exploring dietary approaches like the Mediterranean diet and plant-based diets can provide valuable insights into how food choices can support immune health and overall vitality.

How Intermittent Fasting May Support Immune Function

Intermittent fasting, characterized by cycles of eating and fasting, has gained attention for its potential benefits on various aspects of health, including immune function.

Understanding Intermittent Fasting:

1. **Intermittent Fasting (IF) Basics:** Intermittent fasting is not a specific diet but rather an eating pattern that alternates between periods of eating and fasting. Common approaches include the 16/8 method (16 hours of fasting and an 8-hour eating window) and the 5:2 method (five days of regular eating and two days of significantly reduced calorie intake).

Immune Support Through Intermittent Fasting:

1. **Autophagy:** Intermittent fasting can stimulate a process called autophagy, which is the body's way of cleaning out damaged cells and regenerating new, healthy ones. This process helps optimize the function of immune cells.

2. **Inflammation Reduction:** Intermittent fasting may help reduce chronic inflammation in the body. Chronic inflammation can weaken the immune system, so lowering it can contribute to better immune function.

3. **Cellular Stress Response:** Fasting triggers a mild cellular stress

response, which prompts the body to adapt and become more resilient. This adaptation may extend to immune cells, making them more efficient in responding to threats.

4. **Improved Insulin Sensitivity:** IF can improve insulin sensitivity, potentially reducing the risk of type 2 diabetes. Better blood sugar control is associated with enhanced immune function.

5. **Weight Management:** Intermittent fasting may support weight management by promoting fat loss while preserving muscle mass. Maintaining a healthy weight is beneficial for overall immune health.

Choosing the Right Approach:

1. **Individualized Approach:** Intermittent fasting is not suitable for everyone. It's important to consult with a healthcare professional, especially if you have underlying health conditions or specific dietary needs.

2. **Hydration:** During fasting periods, staying hydrated is essential. Drink plenty of water and herbal teas to maintain overall health.

Questions for Reflection:

1. Are you familiar with the concept of intermittent fasting and its potential benefits for immune health?

2. Have you ever considered or practiced intermittent fasting as part of your dietary routine, and if so, what was your experience?

3. Are you open to exploring intermittent fasting under the guidance of a healthcare professional to potentially support your immune function?

4. Can you envision the long-term impact of intermittent fasting on your overall well-being and immune resilience?

5. How do you feel about incorporating fasting periods into your eating routine to potentially enhance your immune health?

Intermittent fasting is a dietary approach that, when used responsibly and under appropriate guidance, may offer benefits for immune function and overall health.

Customizing Your Diet for Specific Health Goals

One size does not fit all when it comes to nutrition. Tailoring your diet to specific health goals can have a profound impact on your immune health and overall well-being

The Power of Personalization:

1. **Unique Health Goals:** Every individual has unique health goals, whether it's weight management, reducing inflammation, improving energy levels, or enhancing immune function.
2. **Bioindividuality:** The concept of bioindividuality recognizes that what works for one person may not work for another. It's essential to consider your specific needs and preferences.

Customizing for Immune Health:

1. **Assessing Your Needs:** Begin by assessing your current health status and immune function. Consult with a healthcare professional if needed to determine your specific requirements.
2. **Balancing Macronutrients:** Depending on your goals, you may need to adjust the balance of macronutrients (carbohydrates, proteins, fats) in your diet. For instance, athletes may need more protein for muscle repair, while those managing blood sugar may focus on complex carbohydrates.
3. **Incorporating Immune-Boosting Foods:** Tailor your diet to include foods rich in immune-boosting nutrients. For example, if you're vitamin D deficient, consider incorporating more sources like fatty fish or fortified dairy products.
4. **Targeted Supplements:** Depending on your individual needs and potential deficiencies, your healthcare provider may recommend specific supplements to support your immune system.

Setting Specific Goals:

1. **Clear Objectives:** Define clear, achievable health goals related to your immune health. Do you aim to reduce inflammation, boost your body's defense mechanisms, or enhance overall vitality?
2. **Tracking Progress:** Keep a record of your dietary choices and any changes in your health or immune function. This tracking can help you assess the effectiveness of your customized plan.

Professional Guidance:

1. **Consult a Healthcare Professional:** It's advisable to work with a healthcare provider, such as a registered dietitian or nutritionist, to create a customized dietary plan that aligns with your health goals.
2. **Regular Check-Ins:** Periodic check-ins with a healthcare professional can help you fine-tune your diet as your health goals evolve.

Questions for Reflection:

1. Have you considered customizing your diet to align with specific health goals, including immune health?
2. What specific health goals do you have in mind, and how do you believe customization could support them?
3. Are you open to seeking guidance from a healthcare professional to create a tailored dietary plan that supports your immune function?
4. Can you envision the long-term impact of customizing your diet to achieve your health goals and foster a resilient immune system?
5. How do you feel about actively taking charge of your nutrition and making informed choices to optimize your immune health?

Customizing your diet for specific health goals empowers you to take control of your well-being and create a dietary plan that aligns with your unique needs.

The Connection Between Obesity and Immune System Dysfunction

Obesity is a complex health issue with far-reaching consequences, including its impact on immune system function.

Understanding Obesity:

1. **Definition:** Obesity is characterized by an excess accumulation of body fat, often measured by body mass index (BMI). It is a multifaceted condition influenced by genetics, lifestyle, and environmental factors.
2. **Prevalence:** Obesity is a global health concern, with increasing rates in many countries. It affects people of all ages, including children.

The Impact on Immune Function:

1. **Chronic Inflammation:** Obesity is associated with chronic, low-grade inflammation throughout the body. This inflammation can impair immune system function.
2. **Immune Cell Dysfunction:** Obesity can lead to dysfunction in immune cells, including macrophages and T cells. These cells play critical roles in immune responses.
3. **Reduced Vaccine Effectiveness:** Obesity has been linked to reduced vaccine effectiveness, potentially making individuals more susceptible to certain diseases.
4. **Impaired Immune Response:** In cases of infection, obesity can impair the immune system's ability to mount an effective response, leading to more severe illness.

The Role of Diet:

1. **Caloric Excess:** Overconsumption of calories, particularly from highly processed and calorie-dense foods, contributes to obesity. These foods often lack essential nutrients that support immune function.
2. **Poor Dietary Choices:** A diet high in sugar, saturated fats, and refined carbohydrates can exacerbate inflammation and weaken the immune system.

3. **Gut Microbiome:** Obesity is associated with alterations in the gut microbiome. A disrupted gut microbiome can negatively impact immune health.

Prevention and Management:

1. **Healthy Eating Habits:** Adopting a balanced, nutrient-dense diet can help prevent and manage obesity. Focus on whole foods, fruits, vegetables, lean proteins, and healthy fats.
2. **Regular Physical Activity:** Incorporating regular physical activity into your routine can support weight management and improve immune function.
3. **Weight Loss:** For individuals with obesity, weight loss achieved through a combination of diet and exercise can lead to improvements in immune system function.

Questions for Reflection:

1. Are you aware of the connection between obesity and immune system dysfunction?
2. Have you considered how your dietary choices may contribute to obesity or support weight management and immune health?
3. How do you feel about the potential impact of obesity on immune system function and overall health?
4. Are you open to adopting dietary and lifestyle changes to prevent or manage obesity and strengthen your immune system?
5. Can you envision the long-term benefits of a balanced diet and regular physical activity on both your weight and immune resilience?

Understanding the link between obesity and immune system dysfunction underscores the importance of maintaining a healthy weight through dietary choices and lifestyle habits.

Strategies for Maintaining a Balanced Diet in the Long Term

Maintaining a balanced diet over the long term is key to supporting immune health and overall well-being.

The Importance of Long-Term Balance:

1. **Consistency:** Long-term dietary habits have a profound impact on health. Consistently making nutritious choices can bolster immune function and reduce the risk of chronic diseases.
2. **Sustainability:** Sustainable dietary patterns are those you can maintain for a lifetime. Fad diets and extreme restrictions are often unsustainable and can lead to dietary imbalances.

Practical Strategies for Long-Term Balance:

1. **Goal Setting:** Define clear and realistic dietary goals that align with your health objectives. Having a purpose can keep you motivated.
2. **Balanced Meal Planning:** Create balanced meals that incorporate a variety of food groups, including fruits, vegetables, lean proteins, whole grains, and healthy fats.
3. **Portion Control:** Be mindful of portion sizes to prevent overeating. Use smaller plates, and listen to your body's hunger and fullness cues.
4. **Regular Eating Patterns:** Establish regular eating patterns by having meals and snacks at consistent times each day. This can help stabilize blood sugar levels and reduce cravings.
5. **Meal Preparation:** Prepare meals at home whenever possible. Home-cooked meals give you control over ingredients and portion sizes.
6. **Mindful Eating:** Practice mindful eating by savoring each bite, paying attention to hunger and fullness cues, and avoiding distractions during meals.
7. **Moderation, Not Deprivation:** Allow yourself occasional treats and indulgences. Moderation is key to maintaining a balanced diet long term.
8. **Variety:** Embrace a variety of foods to ensure you receive a wide range of nutrients. Experiment with different cuisines and recipes to keep meals exciting.

9. **Gradual Changes:** If you're looking to improve your diet, consider making gradual changes rather than attempting a complete overhaul. Small, sustainable adjustments are more likely to stick.

10. **Seek Support:** Share your dietary goals with friends and family, and consider joining a support group or working with a registered dietitian for guidance and accountability.

Education and Adaptation:

1. **Continuous Learning:** Stay informed about nutrition and its connection to health. Nutritional guidelines and recommendations may evolve, so it's essential to stay up to date.

2. **Adapt to Life Changes:** Be flexible in adapting your diet to life changes, such as aging, pregnancy, or shifts in activity levels. Your dietary needs may evolve over time.

Self-Compassion:

1. **Forgiveness:** If you veer off course or have an occasional indulgence, practice self-compassion and avoid self-criticism. One meal or snack does not define your entire diet.

Questions for Reflection:

1. Are you committed to maintaining a balanced diet in the long term to support your immune health and overall well-being?

2. Have you considered how these practical strategies align with your current dietary habits and goals?

3. How do you envision incorporating these strategies into your daily life to create a sustainable, balanced diet?

4. Are you open to seeking support and guidance, whether from friends, family, or healthcare professionals, in your journey toward a balanced diet?

5. Can you visualize the long-term benefits of maintaining a balanced diet, not only for your immune health but for your overall quality of

life?

Sustaining a balanced diet over the long term is a powerful investment in your health, including the strength of your immune system. As we conclude our exploration in this chapter, you'll have a comprehensive understanding of various dietary patterns and practices to promote immune resilience and lifelong wellness.

Chapter 7: Nutritional Strategies for Aging Gracefully

The Impact of Aging on Immune System Resilience

Aging is a natural and inevitable process, and as we age, our immune system undergoes changes that can influence our overall health.

Understanding the Aging Process:

1. **Natural Progression:** Aging is a complex process marked by gradual changes in the body's structure and function. This includes changes in the immune system, a phenomenon known as immunosenescence.

Immunosenescence and Its Effects:

1. **Immune Decline:** Immunosenescence refers to the gradual decline in the immune system's function. It can lead to a weakened ability to defend against infections and an increased risk of chronic diseases.
2. **Decreased Vaccine Efficacy:** Aging can reduce the effectiveness of vaccines, making older adults more susceptible to vaccine-preventable diseases.
3. **Inflammation:** Aging is often associated with chronic low-grade inflammation, known as inflammaging. This state of chronic inflammation can impair immune responses.
4. **Autoimmune Disorders:** As we age, the risk of autoimmune disorders, where the immune system attacks the body's own tissues, may increase.

The Role of Nutrition in Aging Gracefully:

1. **Nutrient Needs:** Aging individuals may have altered nutrient requirements. For example, the need for certain vitamins and minerals, such as vitamin D and calcium, may increase to support bone health.

2. **Antioxidants:** Antioxidant-rich foods can help combat the effects of oxidative stress and inflammation associated with aging. Berries, leafy greens, and nuts are excellent sources.
3. **Protein:** Adequate protein intake is crucial for maintaining muscle mass and immune function in older adults. Lean meats, fish, dairy, and plant-based protein sources should be included.
4. **Fiber:** A diet rich in fiber supports digestive health, which is vital for nutrient absorption and overall well-being.

Balancing Nutrition and Aging:

1. **Regular Health Check-Ups:** Regular medical check-ups can help identify any nutritional deficiencies or health conditions that may affect dietary needs.
2. **Hydration:** Older adults may have a reduced sensation of thirst, making them more susceptible to dehydration. Staying well-hydrated is essential.
3. **Meal Planning:** Plan meals that are nutritionally dense to ensure you're meeting your dietary needs. This may include consulting with a registered dietitian for guidance.
4. **Supplementation:** In some cases, supplementation may be necessary to address specific nutrient deficiencies. Consult with a healthcare provider before taking any supplements.

Questions for Reflection:

1. Are you aware of the impact of aging on the immune system and overall health?
2. How do you feel about the potential challenges that come with aging and maintaining immune resilience?
3. Have you considered how your dietary choices can play a role in supporting your immune health as you age gracefully?
4. Are you open to adapting your diet to meet changing nutrient needs as you age, including seeking guidance from healthcare professionals?
5. Can you envision the long-term benefits of incorporating immune-

supportive nutrition into your life to age gracefully?

Understanding the impact of aging on the immune system and the role of nutrition in supporting immune health is essential for aging gracefully and maintaining a high quality of life.

Nutritional Needs for Older Adults to Support Immune Health

As we age, our nutritional needs evolve, and it becomes increasingly important to make conscious dietary choices that support immune health.

Understanding the Unique Nutritional Needs of Older Adults:

1. **Changes in Metabolism:** Metabolism tends to slow down with age, which means that older adults may require fewer calories. However, the need for essential nutrients remains high.
2. **Digestive Changes:** Digestive function can change, affecting nutrient absorption. Older adults may experience reduced stomach acid production and absorption efficiency.
3. **Bone Health:** Aging is associated with a greater risk of osteoporosis. Adequate calcium and vitamin D intake is vital for maintaining bone health.
4. **Protein Requirement:** Protein needs may increase to support muscle maintenance and immune function.

Key Nutrients for Immune Health in Older Adults:

1. **Vitamin D:** Adequate vitamin D intake is crucial for older adults as it supports bone health, immunity, and overall well-being. Spend time outdoors and consider vitamin D supplements if recommended by a healthcare provider.
2. **Vitamin C:** Vitamin C is an antioxidant that helps protect cells and supports immune function. Citrus fruits, bell peppers, and broccoli are excellent sources.
3. **Zinc:** Zinc is essential for immune cell function and wound healing. Foods like nuts, seeds, lean meats, and dairy products provide zinc.

4. **Vitamin E:** Vitamin E is an antioxidant that helps maintain immune cell integrity. Nuts, seeds, and vegetable oils are good sources.
5. **Protein:** Protein is necessary for maintaining muscle mass and immune function. Include lean meats, poultry, fish, dairy, and plant-based protein sources in your diet.
6. **Fiber:** A high-fiber diet supports digestive health, which is essential for nutrient absorption and overall well-being.

Hydration: Adequate hydration is critical for older adults, as the sensation of thirst may diminish with age. Dehydration can impact immune function and overall health.

Reducing Sodium: High sodium intake can lead to hypertension, which can affect heart health. Reducing sodium intake can be beneficial for overall well-being.

Antioxidant-Rich Foods: Incorporate antioxidant-rich foods like berries, leafy greens, and nuts to combat oxidative stress associated with aging.

Consulting a Healthcare Provider: Consider discussing your specific nutritional needs with a registered dietitian or healthcare provider to create a dietary plan tailored to your health goals.

Questions for Reflection:

1. Are you aware of the unique nutritional needs of older adults, especially in relation to immune health?
2. How do you feel about making conscious dietary choices to support your immune health as you age?
3. Have you considered how incorporating immune-supportive nutrients into your diet can enhance your overall well-being?
4. Are you open to seeking guidance from healthcare professionals to create a personalized nutrition plan that supports your immune system as you age gracefully?
5. Can you envision the long-term benefits of prioritizing immune-supportive nutrition to maintain a high quality of life in your later

years?

Understanding and meeting the specific nutritional needs of older adults is crucial for supporting immune health and overall well-being as you age gracefully.

Addressing Age-Related Vitamin and Mineral Deficiencies

As we age, our bodies may become less efficient at absorbing and utilizing certain vitamins and minerals. Addressing age-related deficiencies is crucial for maintaining overall health and supporting immune function.

Understanding Age-Related Deficiencies:

1. **Reduced Absorption:** With aging, the digestive system may become less efficient at absorbing essential nutrients, including vitamins and minerals.
2. **Changing Dietary Habits:** Older adults may experience shifts in dietary preferences or reduced food intake, which can impact nutrient intake.
3. **Medication Interactions:** Some medications can interfere with nutrient absorption. It's essential to be aware of potential interactions.

Common Age-Related Deficiencies:

1. **Vitamin D:** Deficiency in vitamin D is common in older adults and can affect immune health, bone health, and overall well-being.
2. **Vitamin B12:** Reduced stomach acid production with age can hinder the absorption of vitamin B12, which is essential for nerve function and blood cell production.
3. **Calcium:** Maintaining strong bones and teeth becomes increasingly important with age. A deficiency in calcium can lead to osteoporosis.
4. **Iron:** Older adults, especially postmenopausal women, may be at risk of iron deficiency anemia. Iron is essential for oxygen transport in the blood.
5. **Vitamin B6:** Vitamin B6 is important for immune function and

cognitive health. Deficiency can lead to anemia and neurological issues.

6. **Folate:** Adequate folate intake is necessary for the production of DNA and RNA. A deficiency can result in anemia and other health problems.

Strategies to Address Deficiencies:

1. **Consult a Healthcare Provider:** If you suspect a deficiency, consult a healthcare provider who can perform blood tests to confirm and provide guidance on supplementation if necessary.
2. **Dietary Adjustments:** Increase your intake of foods rich in the deficient nutrient. For example, consume more vitamin D-rich foods like fatty fish or fortified dairy products.
3. **Supplementation:** If recommended by a healthcare provider, consider taking supplements to address specific deficiencies. Be cautious not to exceed recommended doses.
4. **Medication Review:** Discuss your medications with a healthcare provider to identify any potential interactions that could affect nutrient absorption.
5. **Balanced Diet:** Maintain a balanced diet that includes a variety of nutrient-dense foods to reduce the risk of deficiencies.

Regular Health Check-Ups: Schedule regular health check-ups to monitor your nutrient status and overall well-being, especially as you age.

Questions for Reflection:

1. Are you aware of the common age-related deficiencies in vitamins and minerals and their potential impact on immune health and overall well-being?
2. How do you feel about proactively addressing these deficiencies through dietary adjustments, supplementation, and regular health check-ups?
3. Have you considered discussing your nutrient status with a healthcare

provider to ensure you are meeting your specific needs as you age gracefully?

4. Can you envision the long-term benefits of addressing age-related vitamin and mineral deficiencies for your overall health and immune resilience?

5. Are you open to making necessary dietary and lifestyle changes to optimize your nutrient intake and maintain vitality in your later years?

Addressing age-related vitamin and mineral deficiencies is a proactive step toward maintaining immune health, preventing health issues, and supporting overall well-being as you age gracefully.

The Role of Protein in Maintaining Muscle Mass and Immune Function

Protein is a fundamental nutrient that plays a vital role in maintaining muscle mass and supporting immune function, particularly as we age.

Understanding the Importance of Protein:

1. **Muscle Maintenance:** Protein is essential for building, repairing, and maintaining muscle tissue. This is particularly crucial as muscle mass tends to decrease with age.
2. **Immune Function:** Protein provides the building blocks for immune cells and antibodies, contributing to a robust immune response.

Protein Needs for Older Adults:

1. **Adequate Intake:** Older adults may require a slightly higher intake of protein compared to younger individuals to support muscle preservation and immune health.
2. **Distribution:** Distributing protein intake evenly throughout the day can help maximize muscle protein synthesis and immune support.

Muscle Mass and Immune Function:

1. **Sarcopenia:** Age-related muscle loss, known as sarcopenia, can lead

to decreased strength and mobility. Adequate protein intake helps combat sarcopenia and maintain muscle mass.

2. **Immune Cell Production:** Protein is essential for the production of immune cells, including T cells and antibodies, which play critical roles in the immune response.

Sources of High-Quality Protein:

1. **Lean Meats:** Skinless poultry, lean cuts of beef or pork, and fish are excellent sources of protein.
2. **Dairy Products:** Low-fat or fat-free dairy products provide protein along with essential nutrients like calcium and vitamin D.
3. **Plant-Based Proteins:** Legumes (beans, lentils), tofu, tempeh, and edamame are plant-based sources of protein.
4. **Nuts and Seeds:** Almonds, peanuts, chia seeds, and hemp seeds are protein-rich and provide healthy fats.
5. **Eggs:** Eggs are a versatile source of protein and also contain important nutrients like choline.

Balancing Protein Intake:

1. **Portion Control:** Pay attention to portion sizes to avoid overconsumption of protein, which can strain the kidneys.
2. **Variety:** Incorporate a variety of protein sources into your diet to ensure a broad range of essential amino acids.

Consult a Registered Dietitian: Consider consulting with a registered dietitian to determine your specific protein needs and ensure you are meeting them through your diet.

Questions for Reflection:

1. Are you aware of the critical role that protein plays in maintaining muscle mass and supporting immune function, especially as you age?
2. How do you feel about proactively including high-quality protein sources in your diet to enhance your muscle health and immune

resilience?

3. Have you considered consulting a healthcare professional or registered dietitian to assess your protein needs and make dietary adjustments accordingly?

4. Can you envision the long-term benefits of prioritizing protein intake for both your muscle function and immune health as you age gracefully?

5. Are you open to making dietary changes to optimize your protein intake and support your overall well-being?

Recognizing the significance of protein in maintaining muscle mass and supporting immune function is a vital aspect of aging gracefully and staying healthy in your later years.

Practical Tips for Healthy Eating as You Age

Maintaining a healthy diet as you age is essential for overall well-being and immune health.

1. Prioritize Nutrient-Dense Foods:

- **Choose Whole Foods:** Focus on whole, unprocessed foods such as fruits, vegetables, lean proteins, whole grains, and healthy fats. These foods provide essential nutrients without unnecessary additives.
- **Colorful Plate:** Aim for a colorful plate, as different-colored fruits and vegetables offer a variety of vitamins, minerals, and antioxidants beneficial for immune health.

2. Balanced Meals:

- **Protein at Every Meal:** Include a source of protein in every meal to support muscle maintenance and immune function. Lean meats, fish, eggs, dairy, and plant-based proteins like beans and tofu are excellent options.
- **Fiber-Rich Foods:** Choose foods high in fiber to support digestive health and nutrient absorption. Whole grains, legumes, and fiber-rich

fruits and vegetables should be part of your daily diet.

3. Portion Control:

- **Mindful Eating:** Pay attention to portion sizes and avoid overeating. Listen to your body's hunger and fullness cues.
- **Smaller Plates:** Using smaller plates can help control portion sizes and prevent overconsumption.

4. Hydration:

- **Stay Hydrated:** Drink plenty of water throughout the day, even if you don't always feel thirsty. Dehydration can affect overall health.
- **Limit Sugary Drinks:** Minimize sugary beverages and opt for water, herbal teas, or infused water instead.

5. Dietary Diversity:

- **Varied Diet:** Incorporate a wide range of foods into your diet to ensure you receive a broad spectrum of nutrients.
- **Rotate Proteins:** Alternate protein sources to benefit from various amino acids and nutrients. For example, switch between poultry, fish, and plant-based proteins.

6. Meal Planning:

- **Plan Ahead:** Plan your meals and snacks to ensure they are well-balanced and meet your nutritional needs.
- **Grocery List:** Create a grocery list based on your meal plan to make shopping easier and avoid impulse purchases.

7. Cooking Methods:

- **Healthy Cooking:** Opt for cooking methods like baking, grilling, steaming, and sautéing rather than frying to reduce the intake of unhealthy fats.

- **Herbs and Spices:** Use herbs and spices to flavor your meals instead of relying on excessive salt or sugar.

8. Regular Health Check-Ups:

- **Medical Assessment:** Schedule regular health check-ups to monitor your overall health, including nutrient status, and discuss any dietary concerns with your healthcare provider.

9. Stay Social:

- **Social Eating:** Share meals with friends and family. Social interactions during meals can enhance your overall dining experience and encourage healthier choices.

10. Be Open to Adaptation:

- **Adapt to Changes:** Be flexible in adapting your diet to changes in activity levels, medical conditions, or dietary requirements as you age.

Questions for Reflection:

1. How do you feel about implementing these practical tips for healthy eating into your daily life to support your overall well-being and immune health as you age gracefully?
2. Have you considered how these tips align with your current dietary habits and whether any adjustments are needed?
3. Are you open to seeking guidance from healthcare professionals or registered dietitians to ensure your diet supports your unique health goals as you age?
4. Can you envision the long-term benefits of making informed dietary choices for your immune resilience and quality of life in your later years?

Incorporating these practical tips for healthy eating into your daily routine can contribute to vitality, immune resilience, and overall well-being as you age gracefully.

Chapter 8: Food Safety and Immunity

Ensuring Food Safety to Prevent Foodborne Illnesses

Food safety is paramount for maintaining good health and a strong immune system.

Understanding Foodborne Illnesses:

1. **Common Culprits:** Foodborne illnesses, often caused by harmful bacteria, viruses, or parasites, can lead to symptoms like diarrhea, nausea, vomiting, and fever.
2. **Weakened Immunity:** These illnesses can be particularly severe for individuals with compromised immune systems, including older adults, young children, pregnant women, and those with chronic diseases.

Key Food Safety Measures:

1. **Hand Hygiene:** Properly wash your hands with soap and water before handling food to prevent the spread of harmful pathogens.
2. **Safe Food Handling:** Follow safe food handling practices, such as keeping raw and cooked foods separate, using separate cutting boards for meats and produce, and refrigerating perishable items promptly.
3. **Cooking Temperatures:** Ensure that foods, especially meats, are cooked to the recommended internal temperatures to kill harmful bacteria. Use a food thermometer for accuracy.
4. **Food Storage:** Refrigerate perishable foods promptly to slow the growth of harmful bacteria. Be mindful of expiration dates.
5. **Proper Thawing:** Thaw frozen foods in the refrigerator or under cold, running water to avoid the growth of bacteria.

Safe Sourcing of Food:

1. **Buy from Reputable Sources:** Purchase food items from reputable

stores and suppliers with good food safety practices.

2. **Wash Produce:** Rinse fruits and vegetables thoroughly under running water, even if you plan to peel them, to remove any potential contaminants.

Minimizing Cross-Contamination:

1. **Clean and Sanitize:** Regularly clean and sanitize kitchen surfaces, utensils, and cutting boards to prevent cross-contamination.
2. **Proper Handlings:** Avoid touching your face, nose, or mouth while handling food to reduce the risk of transferring harmful pathogens.

Questions for Reflection:

1. Are you aware of the importance of food safety in preventing foodborne illnesses and its direct impact on your immune health?
2. How do you feel about incorporating these key food safety measures into your daily food preparation and handling routines?
3. Have you considered how your current food safety practices align with these recommendations, and are there areas where improvements can be made?
4. Are you open to taking the necessary steps to ensure food safety and protect your immune system from potential threats posed by foodborne pathogens?
5. Can you envision the long-term benefits of maintaining food safety practices for your overall health and well-being?

Understanding and practicing food safety is essential for preventing foodborne illnesses, protecting your immune health, and maintaining overall well-being.

The Relationship Between Foodborne Infections and Immune Responses

Foodborne infections can have a significant impact on the immune system, as they challenge the body's defense mechanisms.

Understanding Foodborne Infections:

1. **Sources of Contamination:** Foodborne infections occur when food is contaminated with harmful bacteria, viruses, parasites, or other pathogens.
2. **Symptoms:** These infections can lead to a range of symptoms, from mild gastrointestinal discomfort to severe illness, depending on the pathogen involved.
3. **Immune Response Activation:** When pathogens from contaminated food enter the body, the immune system is activated to defend against the threat.

Immune Responses to Foodborne Infections:

1. **Innate Immunity:** The first line of defense involves innate immunity, which includes physical barriers like the stomach's acidic environment and immune cells that quickly respond to pathogens.
2. **Adaptive Immunity:** When the innate immune system is unable to contain the infection, the adaptive immune system is mobilized. This system produces specific antibodies and immune cells to target the invading pathogens.
3. **Inflammation:** In response to infection, the body often initiates an inflammatory response. While inflammation is a natural part of the immune response, chronic inflammation can be detrimental to overall health.
4. **Immune Memory:** After successfully overcoming a foodborne infection, the immune system may develop memory cells that "remember" the pathogen. This can provide immunity against future exposures to the same pathogen.

Impact on Immune Health:

1. **Weakened Immunity:** Foodborne infections can temporarily weaken the immune system as it focuses its resources on fighting the pathogen. This can make individuals more susceptible to other illnesses during the infection.
2. **Long-Term Effects:** Chronic or severe foodborne infections can

have lasting effects on immune health and overall well-being.

Prevention and Recovery:

1. **Rehydration:** In cases of foodborne illness, rehydration is essential to prevent dehydration, which can further compromise immune function.
2. **Rest and Nutrient Intake:** Adequate rest and nourishing foods can support the body's recovery from foodborne infections.

Questions for Reflection:

1. Are you aware of the relationship between foodborne infections and immune responses, and how infections can challenge and impact your immune system?
2. How do you feel about the body's intricate defense mechanisms and its ability to respond to foodborne pathogens?
3. Have you considered the importance of food safety practices in preventing foodborne infections and the potential strain they can place on your immune system?
4. Are you open to adopting food safety measures to reduce the risk of foodborne infections and support your immune health?
5. Can you envision the long-term benefits of maintaining food safety practices to safeguard your immune resilience and overall well-being?

Understanding how foodborne infections trigger immune responses is crucial for appreciating the body's ability to protect itself.

Safe Food Handling Practices in the Kitchen

Maintaining a safe kitchen environment is essential for preventing foodborne illnesses and supporting immune health.

1. Hand Hygiene:

- **Handwashing:** Thoroughly wash your hands with soap and warm water for at least 20 seconds before handling food, after using the restroom, touching pets, or handling raw foods.

- **Fingernail Care:** Keep your fingernails trimmed and clean to prevent the accumulation of dirt and bacteria.

2. Cross-Contamination Prevention:

- **Separation:** Keep raw meats, poultry, and seafood separate from other foods, both in the refrigerator and during meal preparation, to avoid cross-contamination.
- **Color-Coded Cutting Boards:** Use color-coded cutting boards (e.g., red for meat, green for vegetables) to prevent cross-contamination.

3. Food Storage:

- **Refrigeration:** Refrigerate perishable foods at or below 40°F (4°C) to slow the growth of harmful bacteria. Use a thermometer to monitor the refrigerator's temperature.
- **Leftovers:** Store leftovers in airtight containers and consume them within a safe timeframe, typically within 3-4 days.

4. Thorough Cooking:

- **Use a Food Thermometer:** Use a food thermometer to ensure that meats and poultry are cooked to safe internal temperatures. Refer to recommended guidelines for specific temperatures.
- **No Partial Cooking:** Avoid partially cooking food and then finishing it later, as this can allow bacteria to multiply.

5. Safe Defrosting:

- **Refrigeration:** Thaw frozen food in the refrigerator, allowing enough time for safe defrosting.
- **Cold Water Bath:** If needed, thaw food under cold, running water in a sealed bag. Change the water every 30 minutes.

6. Cleaning and Sanitizing:

- **Regular Cleaning:** Routinely clean countertops, cutting boards, utensils, and kitchen equipment with hot, soapy water to remove potential contaminants.
- **Sanitizing:** Use a sanitizing solution on cutting boards and countertops to kill remaining bacteria after cleaning.

7. Proper Disposal:

- **Dispose of Spoiled Food:** Discard any food that appears spoiled, has an off odor, or shows signs of mold.
- **Trash Management:** Ensure proper disposal of food waste to prevent attraction of pests.

8. Safe Handling of Produce:

- **Wash Fruits and Vegetables:** Rinse fruits and vegetables thoroughly under running water, even if you plan to peel them.
- **Avoid Cross-Contamination:** Use a separate cutting board for raw produce and raw meats.

9. Safe Egg Handling:

- **Refrigeration:** Store eggs in their original carton in the refrigerator and use them within three weeks.
- **Cook Eggs Thoroughly:** Cook eggs until both the yolk and white are firm to reduce the risk of salmonella.

10. Stay Informed:

- **Food Recalls:** Stay informed about food recalls and follow guidance from health authorities regarding contaminated products.

Questions for Reflection:

1. How do you feel about incorporating these safe food handling practices into your kitchen routine to prevent foodborne illnesses and protect your immune health?
2. Have you considered the importance of a clean and safe kitchen environment in maintaining overall well-being?
3. Are you open to making changes in your kitchen practices to align with these recommendations and reduce the risk of foodborne infections?
4. Can you envision the long-term benefits of maintaining safe food handling practices to support your immune resilience and overall health?

Practicing safe food handling in your kitchen is a fundamental step toward protecting yourself and your loved ones from foodborne illnesses, thereby supporting immune health and overall well-being.

Avoiding Contaminants and Toxins in Food

Ensuring the purity of the food you consume is critical for safeguarding your immune health.

Understanding Food Contaminants and Toxins:

1. **Contaminants:** Contaminants in food can include harmful microorganisms like bacteria, viruses, and parasites, as well as chemical substances or foreign objects that should not be present.
2. **Toxins:** Foodborne toxins may be naturally occurring, such as those produced by certain molds or bacteria, or they can be introduced through contamination.

Key Measures to Avoid Contaminants and Toxins:

1. Selecting Safe Food Sources:

- **Reputable Suppliers:** Choose food products from reputable suppliers, markets, and stores that adhere to food safety regulations.
- **Check Labels:** Read food labels and be aware of any recalls or

advisories related to specific products.

2. Proper Food Storage:

- **Refrigeration:** Refrigerate perishable foods promptly and at the correct temperature (40°F or 4°C or lower) to slow down bacterial growth.
- **Cooked Food:** Store cooked food separately from raw food to prevent cross-contamination.

3. Safe Food Preparation:

- **Clean Hands and Surfaces:** Practice thorough handwashing and regularly sanitize kitchen surfaces, utensils, and cutting boards.
- **Cook Thoroughly:** Cook meat, poultry, and seafood to safe internal temperatures, using a food thermometer to ensure accuracy.

4. Avoiding Cross-Contamination:

- **Separation:** Keep raw meats and their juices away from other foods to prevent cross-contamination.
- **Proper Thawing:** Thaw frozen foods safely in the refrigerator, not on the countertop.

5. Careful Selection of Produce:

- **Wash Produce:** Thoroughly rinse fruits and vegetables under running water, even if you plan to peel them.
- **Avoid Damaged Produce:** Discard any produce that appears bruised, damaged, or moldy.

6. Be Cautious with Seafood:

- **Selecting Seafood:** Choose seafood from trusted sources and avoid fish that appear spoiled.

- **Mercury Concerns:** Be aware of mercury levels in certain fish and seafood and limit consumption accordingly, especially for vulnerable populations.

7. Awareness of Food Recalls:

- **Stay Informed:** Keep informed about food recalls and advisories, and promptly dispose of any recalled products.

8. Limiting Exposure to Toxins:

- **Mycotoxins:** Be cautious about consuming food items that may contain mycotoxins (toxins produced by molds).

Questions for Reflection:

1. Are you aware of the potential risks associated with food contaminants and toxins and their impact on immune health and overall well-being?
2. How do you feel about adopting these measures to avoid contaminants and toxins in the food you consume, thereby safeguarding your immune resilience?
3. Have you considered the importance of being an informed consumer and staying updated on food recalls and advisories?
4. Are you open to making changes in your food selection, storage, and preparation practices to align with these recommendations and enhance your immune health?
5. Can you envision the long-term benefits of avoiding contaminants and toxins in food for your overall health and well-being?

Taking proactive steps to avoid contaminants and toxins in the food you consume is essential for preserving immune health and promoting overall well-being.

Dietary Precautions During Travel and in Unfamiliar Environments

Maintaining safe dietary practices while traveling or in unfamiliar environments is crucial for protecting your immune health.

1. Research and Planning:

- **Destination Information:** Before traveling, research the destination's food safety standards and common foodborne illnesses. Are there specific risks or precautions you should be aware of?
- **Safe Food Sources:** Identify reputable restaurants and eateries known for their food safety practices. Reading reviews or asking for recommendations can be helpful.

2. Water and Beverage Safety:

- **Bottled Water:** In regions with uncertain water quality, opt for bottled water. Ensure the seal on the bottle is intact.
- **Ice Considerations:** Be cautious with ice in beverages, as it may be made from tap water. Consider asking for drinks without ice.

3. Cooked and Hot Foods:

- **Prioritize Cooking:** Choose foods that are thoroughly cooked and served hot. Avoid raw or undercooked seafood, meats, and eggs.

4. Fresh Produce:

- **Wash Thoroughly:** If consuming raw fruits and vegetables, wash them thoroughly under running water or opt for fruits with peels that can be removed.

5. Street Food Awareness:

- **Local Delicacies:** While street food can offer exciting culinary experiences, exercise caution. Look for vendors with clean and well-maintained stalls.
- **Watch the Preparation:** Observe how the food is prepared, and ensure it's cooked to a safe temperature.

6. Avoiding Tap Water:

- **Oral Hygiene:** Use bottled water for brushing your teeth and avoid accidentally ingesting tap water while showering.

7. Hand Hygiene:

- **Hand Sanitizer:** Carry a hand sanitizer with at least 60% alcohol to use when handwashing facilities are not readily available.

8. Allergy and Dietary Restrictions:

- **Communication:** Clearly communicate any food allergies or dietary restrictions to restaurant staff to prevent accidental exposure to allergens.

9. Medications and Vaccinations:

- **Consult Healthcare Providers:** Depending on your travel destination, consult healthcare providers for vaccinations and medications, including those related to foodborne illnesses.

10. Moderation:

- **Balanced Choices:** While exploring new cuisines is part of the travel experience, strive for a balanced diet. Overindulgence can strain your digestive system.

Questions for Reflection:

1. How do you feel about proactively taking dietary precautions during travel and in unfamiliar environments to protect your immune health and overall well-being?
2. Have you considered the importance of research and planning before embarking on a journey to ensure a safe and enjoyable culinary experience?
3. Are you open to practicing food safety measures, even when trying local delicacies or street food, to reduce the risk of foodborne illnesses?
4. Can you envision the long-term benefits of maintaining dietary

precautions during travel for your overall health and immune resilience?

Implementing these dietary precautions during travel and in unfamiliar environments is essential for safeguarding your immune health and enjoying your adventures to the fullest.

Chapter 9: Immune-Boosting Supplements and Their Controversies

An Overview of Common Immune-Boosting Supplements

Supplements have gained popularity as a means to support immune health, especially during times of heightened concern about illness.

1. Vitamin C:

- **Benefits:** Vitamin C is known for its antioxidant properties, which can help protect immune cells from oxidative damage. It may also stimulate the production and function of white blood cells.
- **Sources:** Citrus fruits, strawberries, kiwi, and supplements.
- **Considerations:** While vitamin C is generally safe, excessive doses can cause gastrointestinal discomfort. It's best to obtain it through a varied diet.

2. Vitamin D:

- **Benefits:** Vitamin D plays a role in immune cell function and helps regulate inflammation. Adequate levels are associated with a reduced risk of respiratory infections.
- **Sources:** Sunlight, fatty fish, fortified foods, and supplements.
- **Considerations:** Consult a healthcare provider to assess your vitamin D levels before taking supplements, as excessive intake can be harmful.

3. Zinc:

- **Benefits:** Zinc is involved in the development and function of immune cells. It may help reduce the duration and severity of colds.
- **Sources:** Meat, dairy, nuts, and supplements.
- **Considerations:** Avoid excessive zinc intake, as it can interfere with

the absorption of other minerals. Stick to recommended doses.

4. Echinacea:

- **Benefits:** Echinacea is an herb believed to stimulate the immune system and reduce the severity of colds.
- **Sources:** Herbal supplements and teas.
- **Considerations:** While some studies suggest potential benefits, more research is needed to confirm its effectiveness.

5. Probiotics:

- **Benefits:** Probiotics, or "good" bacteria, support gut health, which is closely linked to immune function. They may help reduce the risk of respiratory and gastrointestinal infections.
- **Sources:** Fermented foods like yogurt, kefir, and supplements.
- **Considerations:** Choose probiotics with well-documented strains, and consult a healthcare provider for guidance.

6. Elderberry:

- **Benefits:** Elderberry is rich in antioxidants and has been used traditionally to alleviate cold and flu symptoms.
- **Sources:** Elderberry supplements, syrups, and extracts.
- **Considerations:** While elderberry is generally safe, its use in some forms may not be suitable for all individuals. Consult with a healthcare provider.

7. Garlic:

- **Benefits:** Garlic contains compounds with potential immune-boosting properties. It may help reduce the severity and duration of colds.
- **Sources:** Fresh garlic, garlic supplements, and culinary use.
- **Considerations:** Incorporating garlic into your diet can be a flavorful

way to support immune health.

8. Astragalus:

- **Benefits:** Astragalus is an herb used in traditional Chinese medicine to strengthen the immune system.
- **Sources:** Astragalus supplements and herbal remedies.
- **Considerations:** More research is needed to validate its immune-boosting effects.

Questions for Reflection:

1. How do you feel about the availability of immune-boosting supplements and their potential benefits in supporting immune health?
2. Have you considered incorporating certain supplements into your diet to enhance your immune resilience, and if so, have you consulted a healthcare provider for guidance?
3. Are you open to exploring these supplements as part of a well-balanced diet, understanding that dietary choices play a significant role in immune health?

While supplements can be a convenient way to support immune health, it's important to approach them with a balanced perspective.

The Benefits and Risks of Supplementing with Vitamins and Minerals

Supplementing with vitamins and minerals can be a double-edged sword, offering potential benefits while carrying certain risks.

Benefits of Supplementing with Vitamins and Minerals:

1. Addressing Deficiencies:

- **Deficiency Correction:** Supplements can be crucial for addressing specific nutrient deficiencies, which can weaken the immune system.
- **Quick Recovery:** In cases of severe deficiency, supplements can lead

to rapid improvements in immune function.

2. Immune Support:

- **Boosting Immunity:** Certain vitamins and minerals, when taken at appropriate levels, can bolster the immune system's function.
- **Reducing Infection Risk:** Adequate intake of nutrients like vitamin C, D, and zinc may reduce the risk and severity of infections.

3. Convenience:

- **Dietary Gaps:** Supplements can bridge dietary gaps when individuals have limited access to nutrient-rich foods or specific dietary restrictions.
- **Simplicity:** Supplements offer a convenient way to ensure adequate nutrient intake, especially for busy lifestyles.

Risks and Considerations:

1. Nutrient Toxicity:

- **Excess Intake:** Overconsumption of certain vitamins and minerals can lead to toxicity, causing adverse health effects.
- **Vitamin Overdose:** High doses of fat-soluble vitamins like A and D are particularly concerning, as they can accumulate in the body.

2. Imbalance:

- **Disruption of Nutrient Balance:** Taking isolated supplements can disrupt the natural balance of nutrients in the body.
- **Mineral Interference:** Excessive intake of one mineral can interfere with the absorption of others.

3. Absorption Issues:

- **Bioavailability:** Not all supplements are easily absorbed, and their effectiveness can vary.

- **Medication Interactions:** Some medications may interfere with nutrient absorption, making supplementation less effective.

4. Health Risks:

- **Underlying Health Conditions:** Individuals with certain health conditions may be more susceptible to adverse effects from supplements.
- **Allergic Reactions:** Allergic reactions to supplements or their additives can occur in some individuals.

5. Quality Control:

- **Supplement Purity:** Quality control and purity of supplements can vary, leading to potential contamination or ineffectiveness.
- **Unregulated Products:** Not all supplements are rigorously regulated by health authorities.

Questions for Reflection:

1. How do you feel about the potential benefits and risks associated with supplementing with vitamins and minerals to support your immune health?
2. Have you considered the importance of seeking guidance from healthcare providers or registered dietitians when considering supplements to ensure safe and appropriate use?
3. Are you open to exploring a balanced approach to nutrient intake, which includes obtaining vitamins and minerals from whole foods in addition to supplements, to support your overall well-being?

Balancing the potential benefits and risks of supplementing with vitamins and minerals is essential for maintaining optimal immune health and overall well-being.

Herbal Supplements and Their Potential Effects on Immunity

Herbal supplements have a long history of use in traditional medicine systems and are often considered natural options for immune support.

Benefits of Herbal Supplements for Immunity:

1. Immune Modulation:

- **Adaptive Responses:** Some herbal supplements, such as echinacea, astragalus, and elderberry, are believed to help modulate the immune response, potentially making it more effective against infections.
- **Reducing Severity:** Certain herbs may reduce the severity and duration of cold and flu symptoms.

2. Antioxidant Properties:

- **Protection Against Oxidative Stress:** Many herbs are rich in antioxidants, which can help protect immune cells from oxidative damage.
- **Supporting Immune Cells:** Antioxidants like quercetin and catechins found in herbs like green tea may support the function of immune cells.

3. Anti-Inflammatory Effects:

- **Reducing Inflammation:** Some herbs possess anti-inflammatory properties that can help mitigate excessive inflammation, which is associated with immune dysfunction.

4. Respiratory Health:

- **Supporting Respiratory Function:** Herbs like licorice root and thyme are used to support respiratory health and may indirectly aid the immune system in fighting respiratory infections.

Considerations and Risks:

1. Efficacy and Standardization:

- **Limited Scientific Evidence:** The efficacy of many herbal supplements for immune support is based on traditional use rather than robust scientific evidence.
- **Lack of Standardization:** Quality and potency can vary among herbal supplements, making it challenging to predict their effects.

2. Interaction with Medications:

- **Potential Interactions:** Some herbal supplements may interact with medications, impacting their effectiveness or safety.

3. Allergic Reactions:

- **Individual Variability:** Allergic reactions to herbs are possible, and individual responses can vary.

4. Dosage and Duration:

- **Appropriate Use:** Determining the correct dosage and duration of herbal supplements can be challenging and may vary among individuals.

5. Safety and Purity:

- **Quality Control:** The purity and safety of herbal supplements are not always guaranteed, as they are not as strictly regulated as pharmaceuticals.

6. Underlying Health Conditions:

- **Preexisting Conditions:** Individuals with certain health conditions should exercise caution when considering herbal supplements.

Questions for Reflection:

1. How do you feel about the potential benefits and considerations associated with herbal supplements for immune support?
2. Have you considered seeking guidance from a healthcare provider or

herbalist when contemplating the use of herbal supplements to ensure safe and appropriate use?

3. Are you open to exploring a balanced approach to immune support that includes whole foods, lifestyle practices, and, when appropriate, herbal supplements?

Understanding the potential effects and considerations of herbal supplements on immunity is essential for making informed choices about their use.

The Importance of Consulting a Healthcare Professional Before Supplementing

The decision to incorporate supplements into your wellness routine, especially for immune support, should not be taken lightly.

1. Personalized Guidance:

- **Assessment:** Healthcare professionals can assess your individual health status, including any underlying medical conditions or medications you may be taking.
- **Customized Recommendations:** Based on this assessment, they can provide personalized recommendations tailored to your specific needs.

2. Safety Precautions:

- **Identification of Risks:** Healthcare providers can identify potential interactions between supplements and medications you're currently taking, helping to avoid adverse effects.
- **Allergies and Sensitivities:** They can also inquire about any allergies or sensitivities you may have that could impact your ability to tolerate specific supplements.

3. Effective Choices:

- **Efficacy Assessment:** Healthcare professionals can guide you in selecting supplements that have scientific evidence supporting their effectiveness.

- **Optimal Dosage:** They can determine the appropriate dosage and duration of supplementation to achieve your health goals safely.

4. Monitoring and Adjustments:

- **Regular Check-Ins:** Healthcare providers can monitor your progress and make adjustments to your supplement regimen as needed.
- **Preventing Overuse:** Regular check-ins help prevent overuse of certain supplements, which can lead to adverse effects.

5. Health Conditions:

- **Underlying Health Conditions:** If you have underlying health conditions, such as autoimmune disorders or chronic diseases, healthcare professionals can provide specialized guidance on supplement use.

6. Quality and Safety:

- **Identifying Reputable Products:** They can recommend reputable supplement brands known for quality and purity.
- **Safety Monitoring:** Healthcare providers stay informed about potential supplement recalls and safety concerns.

7. Holistic Perspective:

- **Comprehensive Care:** Healthcare professionals consider your overall health and well-being, ensuring that supplement use aligns with your holistic health goals.

Questions for Reflection:

1. How do you feel about the importance of seeking guidance from a healthcare professional before incorporating supplements into your wellness routine, particularly for immune support?
2. Have you considered the potential risks of self-prescribing

supplements without consulting a healthcare provider, including the risk of interactions and adverse effects?

3. Are you open to a holistic approach to immune health that includes professional guidance to ensure safe and effective supplement use?

4. Can you envision the long-term benefits of collaborating with a healthcare professional to support your immune resilience and overall well-being?

The guidance of a healthcare professional is invaluable when it comes to making informed decisions about supplementing for immune health.

Navigating the Controversial Aspects of Supplement Use

The world of supplements is filled with controversy, from conflicting research findings to varying opinions on their efficacy.

1. Conflicting Research:

- **Understanding Varied Studies:** Research on supplements can yield mixed results. Some studies may suggest benefits, while others find no significant effects.
- **Critical Evaluation:** Consider the quality of studies, sample sizes, and the reliability of sources when interpreting research findings.

2. Regulatory Oversight:

- **Lack of Regulation:** Supplements are not as rigorously regulated as pharmaceuticals, leading to concerns about their quality and safety.
- **Vetting Brands:** It's essential to choose reputable supplement brands that adhere to quality control standards.

3. Overuse and Misuse:

- **Self-Prescribing:** Many individuals self-prescribe supplements without professional guidance, potentially leading to overuse or misuse.

- **Consulting Professionals:** Seek guidance from healthcare providers or registered dietitians to avoid unnecessary supplement use.

4. False Claims:

- **Marketing Claims:** Be cautious of supplements that make bold claims without scientific evidence to support them.
- **Critical Thinking:** Exercise critical thinking and fact-checking when evaluating supplement advertisements and testimonials.

5. Interactions and Side Effects:

- **Potential Interactions:** Some supplements can interact with medications or cause side effects, making it crucial to consult healthcare professionals.
- **Monitoring:** Regularly monitor your health when taking supplements to detect any adverse effects promptly.

6. Holistic Health Approach:

- **Balanced Lifestyle:** Remember that supplements are only one aspect of immune health. A balanced lifestyle, including a nutritious diet, regular exercise, and adequate sleep, plays a significant role.

7. Dietary Sources:

- **Whole Foods:** Focus on obtaining nutrients from whole foods whenever possible. Supplements should complement, not replace, a healthy diet.

8. Individual Variability:

- **Personalized Needs:** Recognize that supplement needs can vary greatly among individuals based on factors like age, gender, and overall health.

Questions for Reflection:

1. How do you feel about navigating the controversial aspects of

supplement use, including conflicting research findings, lack of regulation, and the potential for overuse?

2. Have you considered the importance of exercising critical thinking and seeking professional guidance when contemplating supplements, particularly for immune support?

3. Are you open to embracing a holistic approach to immune health, understanding that supplements should be integrated into a comprehensive wellness strategy?

4. Can you envision the long-term benefits of informed decision-making and a balanced perspective when it comes to supplement use for immune resilience and overall well-being?

Navigating the controversies surrounding supplement use requires a discerning and informed approach.

Chapter 10: Putting Knowledge into Practice: Meal Plans and Recipes

Creating Immune-Boosting Meal Plans for Different Dietary Preferences

In this final chapter, we'll put our knowledge into action by crafting immune-boosting meal plans that cater to various dietary preferences. These meal plans will help you translate the insights gained throughout this book into practical, everyday choices that support your immune health.

Meal Plan 1: Plant-Based Immune Support

Breakfast:

- **Smoothie:** Blend spinach, banana, berries, chia seeds, and almond milk for a nutrient-packed start.

Lunch:

- **Quinoa Salad:** Combine cooked quinoa with chickpeas, mixed vegetables, and a lemon-tahini dressing.

Snack:

- **Mixed Nuts:** Enjoy a handful of mixed nuts for a dose of healthy fats and antioxidants.

Dinner:

- **Stir-Fried Tofu:** Sauté tofu with broccoli, bell peppers, and a ginger-garlic sauce. Serve with brown rice.

Meal Plan 2: Mediterranean Immune Boost

Breakfast:

- **Greek Yogurt Parfait:** Layer Greek yogurt with honey, fresh berries, and a sprinkle of granola.

Lunch:

- **Mediterranean Salad:** Toss together cucumbers, tomatoes, olives, feta cheese, and a drizzle of olive oil and balsamic vinegar.

Snack:

- **Hummus and Veggies:** Dip sliced carrots, cucumbers, and bell peppers in hummus.

Dinner:

- **Grilled Salmon:** Grill salmon with a lemon-herb marinade. Serve with quinoa and roasted asparagus.

Meal Plan 3: Balanced Omnivore's Immunity

Breakfast:

- **Oatmeal:** Top your oatmeal with sliced bananas, nuts, and a drizzle of honey.

Lunch:

- **Chicken and Vegetable Wrap:** Fill a whole-grain wrap with grilled chicken, mixed greens, and a light yogurt dressing.

Snack:

- **Apple Slices and Peanut Butter:** Enjoy a classic combo for a quick energy boost.

Dinner:

- **Lean Beef Stir-Fry:** Stir-fry lean beef with broccoli, snap peas, and a low-sodium teriyaki sauce. Serve over brown rice.

Meal Plan 4: Gluten-Free and Immunity-Focused

Breakfast:

- **Chia Seed Pudding:** Mix chia seeds with almond milk and top with sliced kiwi and a drizzle of honey.

Lunch:

- **Quinoa and Black Bean Bowl:** Combine cooked quinoa with black beans, corn, avocado, and a lime-cilantro dressing.

Snack:

- **Rice Cakes with Avocado:** Spread mashed avocado on rice cakes and sprinkle with black pepper.

Dinner:

- **Grilled Chicken and Vegetables:** Grill chicken breast alongside zucchini, red onions, and cherry tomatoes. Serve with a side of quinoa.

Questions for Reflection:

1. Which of these meal plans aligns most closely with your dietary preferences, and do you feel inspired to try it for immune support?
2. Have you considered the importance of incorporating a variety of immune-boosting foods into your daily meals?
3. Are you open to experimenting with these meal plans as part of your commitment to immune health and overall well-being?

These meal plans are designed to help you put your newfound knowledge about nutrition and immune health into practice. By tailoring your meals to your dietary preferences, you can support your immune system while savoring delicious and nourishing dishes. As we conclude our journey, remember that a balanced, nutrient-rich diet is a key foundation for a resilient immune system and a vibrant life.

Immune-Supportive Recipes and Cooking Techniques

In this chapter, we'll dive into a selection of immune-supportive recipes and cooking techniques that incorporate the principles discussed throughout this book. These recipes will not only boost your immune system but also tantalize your taste buds with delicious, healthful dishes.

Recipe 1: Immunity-Boosting Green Smoothie

Ingredients:

- 1 cup spinach or kale
- 1 ripe banana
- 1/2 cup mixed berries (e.g., blueberries, strawberries)
- 1 tablespoon chia seeds
- 1 cup almond milk (or your preferred plant-based milk)

Instructions:

1. Place all ingredients in a blender.
2. Blend until smooth and creamy.
3. Pour into a glass and enjoy as a refreshing and nutrient-packed breakfast or snack.

Recipe 2: Lemon-Garlic Roasted Chicken

Ingredients:

- 4 boneless, skinless chicken breasts
- 4 cloves garlic, minced
- 2 lemons, zested and juiced
- 2 tablespoons olive oil
- 1 teaspoon dried oregano
- Salt and pepper to taste

Instructions:

1. Preheat your oven to 375°F (190°C).
2. In a bowl, combine minced garlic, lemon zest, lemon juice, olive oil, oregano, salt, and pepper.
3. Place the chicken breasts in a baking dish and pour the lemon-garlic

mixture over them.

4. Roast in the oven for 25-30 minutes, or until the chicken reaches an internal temperature of 165°F (74°C).
5. Serve with a side of steamed broccoli and quinoa for a complete immune-supportive meal.

Recipe 3: Berry and Almond Overnight Oats

Ingredients:

- 1/2 cup rolled oats
- 1 cup almond milk (or your preferred milk)
- 1/4 cup mixed berries (e.g., raspberries, blackberries)
- 2 tablespoons almond butter
- 1 tablespoon honey or maple syrup (optional)
- Chopped almonds for garnish (optional)

Instructions:

1. In a mason jar or container, combine rolled oats and almond milk.
2. Add the mixed berries, almond butter, and honey or maple syrup if desired.
3. Stir well to combine, ensuring the almond butter is evenly distributed.
4. Seal the jar and refrigerate overnight.
5. In the morning, give the oats a good stir and top with chopped almonds for an extra crunch.

Cooking Techniques for Immune-Supportive Meals:

1. Sauté with Garlic and Onions:

- Garlic and onions contain immune-boosting compounds. Sauté them as a flavorful base for soups, stews, and stir-fries.

2. Use Herbs and Spices:

- Incorporate immune-boosting herbs and spices like ginger, turmeric, and oregano into your cooking to add flavor and health benefits.

3. Include Fermented Foods:

- Fermented foods like yogurt, kimchi, and sauerkraut support gut health, which is closely linked to immune function.

4. Choose Whole Grains:

- Opt for whole grains like brown rice, quinoa, and whole wheat pasta to provide your body with essential nutrients and fiber.

5. Roast Colorful Vegetables:

- Roasting vegetables like sweet potatoes, carrots, and bell peppers intensifies their flavors and enhances their nutritional value.

Questions for Reflection:

1. Which of these immune-supportive recipes are you excited to try, and why?
2. Have you considered the importance of incorporating immune-boosting ingredients and cooking techniques into your daily meals to enhance your immune health?
3. Are you open to experimenting with these recipes and techniques as part of your commitment to nourishing your immune system and overall well-being?

These immune-supportive recipes and cooking techniques empower you to infuse your meals with flavor and health benefits. By incorporating these practices into your daily culinary routine, you can savor the taste of wellness while strengthening your immune system. As we conclude our journey, remember that a balanced, nutrient-rich diet is a key foundation for a resilient immune system and a vibrant life.

Tips for Incorporating Immune-Boosting Foods into Daily Meals

Creating meals that support your immune system doesn't have to be complicated or overwhelming. In this section, we'll provide practical tips to seamlessly integrate immune-boosting foods into your daily meals, making healthy eating a sustainable and enjoyable habit.

1. Start Your Day with a Nutrient-Packed Breakfast:

- **Fruit and Yogurt:** Top your morning yogurt with a mix of fresh berries, which are rich in antioxidants, and a drizzle of honey.
- **Oatmeal:** Stir in sliced bananas or chopped apples for added vitamins and fiber.

2. Power Up with Leafy Greens:

- **Salads:** Add spinach, kale, or arugula as a base for your salads. These greens are packed with vitamins and minerals.
- **Smoothies:** Sneak a handful of spinach or kale into your morning smoothie for an extra nutritional punch.

3. Load Up on Colorful Vegetables:

- **Stir-Fries:** Incorporate a variety of colorful vegetables like bell peppers, broccoli, and carrots into your stir-fry dishes.
- **Roasted Veggies:** Roast vegetables like sweet potatoes, Brussels sprouts, and cauliflower with olive oil and your favorite seasonings.

4. Include Lean Proteins:

- **Chicken and Turkey:** Opt for lean poultry options, like chicken and turkey, in your meals. They provide essential amino acids for a strong immune system.
- **Fish:** Incorporate fatty fish like salmon and trout, which are rich in omega-3 fatty acids that support immune function.

5. Don't Forget the Healthy Fats:

- **Avocado:** Add slices of avocado to your sandwiches and salads to increase your intake of healthy monounsaturated fats.
- **Nuts and Seeds:** Sprinkle nuts and seeds, such as almonds and flaxseeds, on top of yogurt or oatmeal.

6. Embrace Whole Grains:

- **Whole Wheat:** Swap out refined grains for whole wheat options like whole grain bread and pasta.
- **Quinoa:** Use quinoa as a versatile base for salads and grain bowls.

7. Prioritize Gut-Healthy Foods:

- **Yogurt:** Incorporate probiotic-rich yogurt into your daily meals to support gut health and immunity.
- **Kombucha:** Enjoy a glass of kombucha as a refreshing and probiotic-rich beverage.

8. Stay Hydrated:

- **Water:** Ensure you stay hydrated throughout the day, as proper hydration supports overall health and immune function.

9. Snack Smart:

- **Fruit:** Keep a bowl of fresh fruit on your kitchen counter for easy snacking.
- **Veggies and Hummus:** Slice up bell peppers, cucumbers, and carrots to dip in hummus for a nutritious snack.

10. Plan Ahead:

- **Meal Prep:** Dedicate time to plan and prepare meals in advance to make healthy eating more convenient.

Questions for Reflection:

1. Which of these tips for incorporating immune-boosting foods into your daily meals resonates with you the most, and how do you plan to implement it into your routine?
2. Have you considered the significance of small, consistent dietary changes in supporting your immune health and overall well-being?
3. Are you open to embracing a gradual, sustainable approach to nourishing your immune system through daily food choices?

Incorporating immune-boosting foods into your daily meals doesn't have to be complex or daunting. By following these practical tips and gradually introducing them into your routine, you can foster a sustainable and nourishing relationship with your immune health. Remember that small, consistent efforts can lead to significant long-term benefits.

Celebrating the Journey Toward Better Immune Health Through Nutrition

Embarking on a journey to enhance your immune health through nutrition is a remarkable and transformative endeavor. In this section, we'll emphasize the importance of celebrating your progress and the positive impact your choices have on your overall well-being.

1. Reflect on Your Achievements:

- **Gratitude:** Take a moment to appreciate the steps you've taken to prioritize your immune health.
- **Journaling:** Consider keeping a journal to document your dietary changes and how they make you feel.

2. Share Your Success:

- **Community:** Share your journey with friends and family. Encourage them to join you in embracing immune-boosting nutrition.
- **Support Network:** Engage with online communities or support groups focused on nutrition and well-being.

3. Small Wins Matter:

- **Acknowledge Progress:** Celebrate even the smallest victories, like consistently incorporating more vegetables into your meals or choosing whole grains over refined ones.
- **Positive Reinforcement:** Recognize that these small wins are building blocks for long-term success.

4. Explore New Flavors:

- **Culinary Adventures:** Experiment with new ingredients and recipes. Embrace the excitement of discovering delicious, immune-boosting dishes.
- **Food Diversity:** Celebrate the diversity of flavors and cultures represented in your meals.

5. Mindful Eating:

- **Savor Each Bite:** Practice mindful eating by savoring the taste, texture, and aroma of your meals.
- **Gratitude Ritual:** Consider saying a simple thank-you before each meal to express gratitude for the nourishment it provides.

6. Wellness Milestones:

- **Health Improvements:** Celebrate improvements in your health, such as increased energy, better digestion, or fewer sick days.
- **Fitness Goals:** If you're pursuing fitness goals alongside your dietary changes, recognize your achievements in strength, endurance, or flexibility.

7. Treat Yourself Occasionally:

- **Balanced Indulgence:** Occasionally enjoy a favorite treat or meal without guilt. Balance is key to maintaining a sustainable approach to nutrition.

8. Educate and Inspire Others:

- **Share Knowledge:** Share your newfound knowledge about immune-boosting nutrition with others.
- **Inspire Change:** Inspire those around you to make healthier food choices and prioritize their immune health.

Questions for Reflection:

1. How do you envision celebrating your journey toward better immune health through nutrition and making it a positive and uplifting experience?
2. Have you considered the significance of gratitude, mindfulness, and sharing your successes with others as integral parts of your wellness journey?
3. Are you open to embracing the joy of culinary exploration and using food as a source of both nourishment and celebration?

Celebrating your journey toward better immune health through nutrition transforms it into a fulfilling and empowering endeavor. By savoring each step, appreciating your progress, and sharing your experiences with others, you not only enhance your own well-being but also inspire positive change in those around you. Remember that the path to better immune health is a journey worth celebrating.

Plea for Reviews:

Dear Reader,

Thank you for choosing "Nutrition and Immune Health" as your guide to a healthier, more resilient life. Your support means the world to us, and we hope the knowledge and insights shared in this book empower you on your journey.

If you found this book valuable, we kindly request your assistance in spreading the word. Reviews from readers like you are incredibly valuable. They help others discover the book and understand its impact.

Please consider leaving an honest review on your favorite platform, whether it's a few words or a detailed reflection of your experience. Your review can inspire and guide fellow readers on their quest for better immune health.

As a token of our gratitude, we invite you to reach out with any questions or comments. Your feedback is invaluable and helps us continue to improve and provide the best possible support.

Thank you for being a part of this journey toward better immune health through nutrition. Together, we can create a healthier and more vibrant world.

With warm regards,

Gabriella Goldberger

Don't miss out!

Visit the website below and you can sign up to receive emails whenever Gabriella Goldberger publishes a new book. There's no charge and no obligation.

https://books2read.com/r/B-A-CNJAB-HFWNC

BOOKS 2 READ

Connecting independent readers to independent writers.